THE REVENGE OF
Anguished English

Also by Richard Lederer

Adventures of a Verbivore

Anguished English

Basic Verbal Skills (with Phillip Burnham)

The Giant Book of Animal Jokes (with James Ertner)

The Bride of Anguished English

The Circus of Words

Comma Sense (with John Shore)

Crazy English

The Cunning Linguist

Fractured English

Get Thee to a Punnery

Have a Punny Christmas

Literary Trivia (with Michael Gilleland)

A Man of My Words

The Miracle of Language

More Anguished English

The Play of Words

Pun & Games

Puns Spooken Here

Sleeping Dogs Don't Lay (with Richard Dowis)

The Word Circus

Word Play Crosswords, volumes 1 and 2 (with Gayle Dean)

The Write Way (with Richard Dowis)

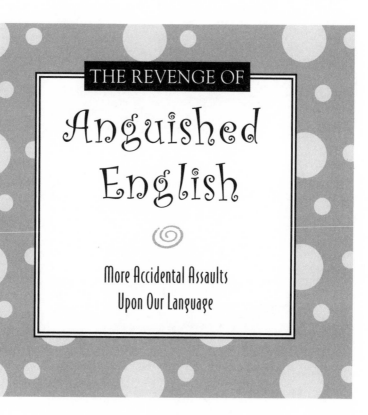

THE REVENGE OF

Anguished English

More Accidental Assaults
Upon Our Language

Richard Lederer

Illustrations by Jim McLean

St. Martin's Press ✙ New York

I am grateful for permission to use about a half-dozen examples from each of the following sources: Norman Sperling's *What Your Anatomy Teacher Won't Tell You,* Charles Sevilla's *Disorder in the Court,* and (with Rodney Jones and Gerald Uelemen) *Disorderly Conduct,* and Don Hauptman's articles in *Word Ways.*

www.stmartins.com

Book design by Ellen Cipriano

Library of Congress Cataloging-in-Publication Data

Lederer, Richard, 1938–
     The revenge of anguished English : more accidental assaults upon our language / Richard Lederer ; illustrations by Jim McLean.—1st U.S. ed.
         p. cm.
     ISBN 0-312-33493-1
     EAN 978-0312-33493-2
         1. English language—Errors of usage—Humor. I. Title.

PN6231.E74L45 2005
428'.002'07—dc22

                                                                                        2004051153

First Edition: April 2005

10 9 8 7 6 5 4 3 2 1

To Martha Barnette,
my radio-active partner

Contents

The Gift of Gaffes

The Power of the Press

Lost in Translation

Eh, What's That You Say?

Introduction

One of the immortal, classic lines in the history of film comedy emerges from the preternaturally large mouth of Joe E. Brown. At the end of *Some Like It Hot,* Brown proposes marriage to Jack Lemmon, who has been masquerading as a female musician throughout their courtship:

> **LEMMON**: Osgood, I'm gonna level with you. We can't get married at all.
> **BROWN**: Why?
> **LEMMON**: Well, in the first place, I'm not a natural blonde.
> **BROWN**: Doesn't matter.
> **LEMMON**: For three years I've been living with a saxophone player.
> **BROWN**: I forgive you.
> **LEMMON**: I can never have children.
> **BROWN**: We can adopt some.
> **LEMMON**: But you don't understand, Osgood. I'm a man!

To which Joe E. Brown answers: "Oh well, nobody's perfect!"

How true. Nobody is perfect, especially in speaking and writing Standard English, which nobody in the world actually does speak and write perfectly. Everybody, no matter how blessed with vocabulary, will at one time or another eat their words and gag on their inadvertent gag. Everybody, whether fine or tin of ear, will occasionally mishear and then misrepeat a word or phrase. Everybody, no matter how well schooled in grammar, will every once in a while misplace a modifier or dangle a participle in public.

And how can anyone be expected not to? The English language contains almost a million words, five times the highest number of words found in any other tongue. Add to that numbing number the vast array of the language's idiosyncratic idioms, along with its myriad words with multiple meanings, kaleidoscopic collage of colorful colloquialisms, and taxing syntax, and it's a wonder any of us ever dares to utter so much as a simple "Hello!"

But dare we do, because language is a gift to be used—even at the risk of being abused. Not that any speaker or writer purposely makes mistakes, of course. We all wish to avoid tripping on our own tongues. Given a choice of how to speak, we all elect eloquent, electrifying elocution. We all strive to write right, right?

Despite the ever-present possibility of structural collapse or grammatical gaffes, we plunge ahead. We know that if, in our desire to communicate, we inadvertently select a malappropriate word or subject a subject to something subjectively substandard, no one's the worse for it. Despite the specter of anguished English, we don't let our language languish. And, as my legions of super-duper blooper snoopers (troopers, all!) know, sometimes a tangled tongue or a word that should be herded back into its pen can bring the world what it can never really get enough of—a good reason to laugh.

Bloopers are that rarest of rarities: true mistakes that are truly funny. In regular life, mishaps are usually too harrowing to be hilarious:

You thought your car was in "Drive" when it was, in fact, in "Reverse." Looking straight ahead, you press on the gas pedal—not funny.

You brush your teeth with rash ointment—not funny.

You're a dentist, and you're moving in with the drill. You sneeze—*extremely* unfunny.

But consider these beguiling boo-boos:

- In an essay, a student wrote, "In 1957, Eugene O'Neill won a Pullet Surprise."
- Many gas stations equipped with snack stores display the sign "Eat Here and Get Gas."
- A headline blared GRANDMOTHER OF EIGHT MAKES HOLE IN ONE.
- A newspaper informed its readers that "the license fee for altered dogs with a certificate will be three dollars, and for pets owned by senior citizens who have not been altered the fee will be a dollar-fifty."
- A classified ad offered "antique desk suitable for lady with thick legs and large drawers."
- During the course of a Gemini flight broadcast, Frank McGhee of NBC News reported: "I have just learned that we do have the film of the astronaut's breakfast, which should be coming up shortly."
- A letter to the editor complained, "It is scandalous to see society women going about with a poodle dog on the end of a leash where a baby would be more fitting."
- A letter from a bank explained, "The adoption of the bank's new name requires no action on your part. Just continue using your present checks and other forms until exhausted."
- On the *Joey Bishop Show*, Joey asked Sen. Barry Goldwater if he would like to be on the show twice a week. The senator answered, "I'd much rather watch you in bed with my wife."

See? A wiggle of a word, a swerve of a typing finger, a tangle of the tongue—and suddenly the world brightens, and you're enjoying a gleeful, guilt-free guffaw! Good for you!

And it is indeed good for you. Increasingly doctors are coming to believe that laughter just might really be the very best medicine of all. In *Anatomy of an Illness*, Norman Cousins shows how he overcame a painful and crippling arthritic disease through humor. "I made the joyous discovery that ten minutes of genuine belly laughter had an anesthetic effect and would give me at least two hours of pain-free sleep," Cousins writes. "Laughter is an ambassador to all the positive emotions," he concludes.

Each year the evidence grows that ingesting humor does a body good. Laughter colors the cheeks, puffs up the lungs, firms the muscles, fortifies the immune system, stabilizes blood sugar levels, adds endorphins to the brain and T cells to the immune system, aerates the capillaries, reduces stress hormones and toxins, dulls pain and inflammation, and tickles the funny bone. "A good laugh and a long sleep are the two best cures," winks an Irish proverb.

Dr. William Fry, a researcher into the beneficial effects of humor, estimates that laughing hard a hundred times provides a physiological effect similar to that produced by working out on a rowing machine for ten minutes. Laughter can be as healthful as jogging, and you don't have to don a sweat suit and go outdoors.

Laughter is also an elixir for the mind. Tests administered before and after humor therapy reveal a reduction of stress and depression and a heightened sense of well-being and creativity. More and more, science is discovering that it hurts only when we *don't* laugh. "Laughter is to life what shock absorbers are to automobiles. It won't take the potholes out of the road, but it sure makes the ride smoother," observes Barbara Johnson. "The most wasted of all days is one without laughter," adds the magician of poetry, e. e. cummings. And more than a century ago, Victor Hugo observed, "Laughter is the sun that drives winter from the human face."

In a recent *AARP* interview, U.N. secretary-general Kofi Annan was asked, "And what is the single greatest thing that sustains you?"

His answer: "A sense of humor. And I laugh at myself."

"Humor is not a trick," writes author and *Prarie Home Companion* host Garrison Keillor. "Humor is a presence in the world—like grace—and shines on everybody." The late and beloved humorist Erma Bombeck, whose column "At Wit's End" was read by millions, speaks to us today: "Laughter rises out of tragedy, when you need it the most, and rewards you for your courage." And the also late and beloved humorist Richard Armour observed, "Comedy, I think, is as high an art as tragedy. It is as important to make people laugh as to make people cry." As bread is the staff of life, laughter is its nectar. Ripples of laughter will wash the brightest pearls onto the shores of your life. Laughter makes life the merriest of go-rounds and will keep you from getting dizzy.

In each introduction of my *Anguished English* books, I have published testimonials about the beneficial effects of the humor winking out from the pages that form the series. In the spirit of that tradition, I offer two recent statements. I don't claim that these reflect everyone's experience with the series, but I have been button-burstingly proud of the joy dispensed by the bloopers I have assembled:

• Several years ago, I was diagnosed with leukemia and went into the hospital for lots of intense chemotherapy. While there, I learned about Norman Cousins's experiences with disease and started dosing myself with humor therapy—Daffy and Bugs, Calvin and Hobbs, Gary Larson, Jeff McNelly, among others. Then someone gave me *Anguished English*. Its history of the world made me laugh like very few other things have, before or since.

I was home between chemo sessions at the time, and my wife, soaking in the tub down the hall, was afraid I would have a seizure. In a time when I desperately needed to laugh, you came through. I am forever grateful. I'm also in complete remission, and have been for almost 14 years. Many thanks.

—*Dean Whitlock, Thetford Center, Vermont*

• The drive to work that morning was stormy but in a strange way. Something was not right. I had the local weather on the television before school started, and I knew conditions were right for a tornado. Students arrived at their first class of the day, and my ninth-grade English class got started on the day's activity. About ten minutes into the period, a tornado warning was issued over our PA system. Being on the first floor of the school meant we stayed in our classroom but we had to sit on the floor close to an interior wall. Students pushed desks out of the way and huddled together in their new seating.

Before joining my students on the floor, I grabbed *Anguished English*. I had already shared the insurance and school note bloopers as read-alouds. The students usually laugh so loudly that I will only share *Anguished English* with them at the end of class so that we can get what we need to get done during class. I thought another section or two would help alleviate any fears or concerns the students might have about the unpredictable weather.

I read from "Two-Headed Headlines" and the section on funny signs. They wanted more. So I turned to the beginning, to the history of the world according to student bloopers. We sat on the floor for most of the class period, and the students were attentive and laughing.

Keep in mind that this was an average-size class of 26 students. Finally, the PA crackled with an all clear. Students let out a groan and didn't get up to return to their seats. Murmurs of "That was fun" and, "I don't want the tornado drill to end" filled the room.

As it turned out, a small tornado did touch down that morning just a few miles away, tearing up a local marina. Nobody was hurt. And I still have students stop by to reminisce about the morning of the tornado and the great fun we had.

Students. Go figure.

—*Lisa Rehm, West Shore Junior/Senior High School,*
Melbourne, Florida

The Renaissance man Francis Bacon once wrote, "Some books are to be tasted, others to be swallowed, and a few to be chewed and digested." This book is to be wolfed down, but, as a protection to you, the consumer, I advise wolfing only one chapter at a time.

If you'd like to share your super-duper bloopers with me, please wing them to richard.lederer@pobox.com.

—Richard Lederer
San Diego, California

THE REVENGE OF
Anguished English

I Kid You Not

"Jennifer, what sound does a mouse make?"
"Er . . . , it goes . . . click!"

Oh, You Kids!

Children are so alive to the possibilities of language and see words and phrases and life itself in startling, fresh ways. A quadriplegic friend of mine tells the story of a time that a little girl saw him coming down a hallway in his wheelchair and exclaimed, "Look, Mommy. There's a man with round feet!" Mother blushed crimson with embarrassment and tried to silence her daughter. But my friend was not at all offended—rather, he was delighted by the girl's linguistic imagination.

A child looks at his grandmother's varicose veins and wonders why "she has lightning in her legs." Another child gazes at a crescent moon and observes, "The moon is just waking up." "Close the curtains," requests a two-year-old girl, sitting in a pool of bright light. "The sun's looking at me too hard." A two-and-a-half-year-old looking at the stars dancing across the black night sky says, more wisely than she can know, "Mommy, that's God's big dot-to-dot."

A first-grader explains that because her principal is female, she's really a "princessipal." A six-year-old boy jumps up on a kitchen sink and exclaims, "Mommy, Daddy, I'm sink-ing!" Small children sometimes call a tongue depressor an "ah-stick" and a sliding board a "whee-down." A little boy sees twins in a baby carriage and says to his mother, "Look there's a baby—and there's a co-baby!"

The poet Carl Sandburg quotes a lad who had just pulled up a large weed from the soil. When his mother said, "My, you were strong to get that out!" the boy answered, "I sure was. The whole earth had hold of it!"

The pearls of wisdom and imagination that fall from the mouths of babes are the most charming and innocent bloopers I receive from my readers. I view these "kiddisms" as bloopers-in-training, and I'm confident that when the boys and girls grow up, they will unknowingly contribute more sophisticated and loopy goofs to my books.

Now sit back and enjoy the latest and freshest batch of kiddisms:

• One day a little girl was sitting and watching her mother do the dishes at the kitchen sink. She suddenly noticed that her mother had several strands of white hair sticking out in contrast on her brunette head. She looked at her mother and inquisitively asked, "Why are some of your hairs white, Mom?"

Her mother replied, "Well, every time you do something wrong and make me cry, one of my hairs turns white."

The little girl thought about this revelation for a while and then asked, "Momma, how come ALL of grandma's hairs are white?"

• A little boy watched, fascinated, as his mother gently rubbed cold cream on her face. "Why are you rubbing cold cream on you face, Mommy?" he asked.

"To make myself beautiful," said his mother. A few minutes later, she began removing the cream with a tissue.

"What's the matter?" he asked. "Are you giving up?"

• A two-and-a-half-year-old walked into the bathroom while her mother was putting on makeup. "I'm going to look just like you, Mommy!" she announced.

"Maybe, when you grow up," her mother told her.

"No, Mommy, tomorrow. I just put on that Oil of Old Lady you always use."

• A little boy asked, "Grandma, do you know how you and God are alike?"

Grandmother mentally polished her halo as she asked, "No, how are we alike?"

"You're both old," he replied.

• Attending a wedding for the first time, a little girl whispered to her mother, "Why is the bride dressed in white?"

"Because white is the color of happiness, and today is the happiest day of her life."

The child thought about this for a moment, then said, "So why is the groom wearing black?"

• After driving for 15 hours, a family was looking for a place to spend the night. At four different motels they saw "Sorry, No Vacancies" signs. Heading back to the car, the seven-year-old asked, "Mom, are we Vacancies?"

• When the bus stopped to pick up Chris for preschool, the bus driver noticed an older woman hugging him as he left the house.

"Is that your grandmother?" the driver asked.

"Yes," Chris said. "She's come to visit us for Christmas."

"How nice," the driver said. "Where does she live?"

"At the airport," Chris replied. "Whenever we want her, we just go out there and get her."

• When asked what he wanted for lunch, three-year-old Stephen, said, "Jumping bread!"

Everyone was puzzled until he pointed to the toaster and said again, "I want jumping bread!"

• As a little girl climbed onto Santa's lap, Santa asked the usual, "And what would you like for Christmas?"

The child stared at him openmouthed for a minute, then gasped, "Didn't you get my e-mail?"

• One summer evening during a violent thunderstorm, a mother was tucking her small boy into bed. She was about to turn off the light when he asked with a tremor in his voice, "Mommy, will you sleep with me tonight?"

The mother smiled and gave him a reassuring hug. "I can't, dear," she said. "I have to sleep in Daddy's room."

A long silence was broken at last by his shaky little voice: "The big sissy."

• On the way to preschool, the doctor had left her stethoscope on the car seat, and her little girl picked it up and began playing with it. *Be still, my heart*, thought the doctor. *My daughter wants to follow in my footsteps.*

Then the child spoke into the instrument: "Welcome to McDonald's. May I take your order?"

• The computer age has gone too far. When a father said, "Amen" after grace one night at the dinner table, one of his children asked what "amen" meant. Before his wife or he could answer, their five-year-old responded: "It means 'send.'"

• Impressed by her five-year-old's vocabulary, Mother complimented the young scholar, who nonchalantly responded, "I have words in my head I haven't even used yet."

• A mother was walking down a city street at night with her five-year-old son. They passed a trio of "ladies of the evening" clad in their skimpy shorts and stockings. The little boy asked his mom, "Mommy, are they moon bathers?"

• Mother informed her son, Brian, that she was going outside to get a little sun. "But Mommy," he gulped, "you already have a son. Me!"

• As mother and son sat on the beach, a well-proportioned woman walked by. "Look, Mom!" exclaimed the little boy. "That lady has on the same swimsuit as you, but hers has a different shape!"

• Hearing her mother reminisce about her old record collection of 45s, a little girl said, "Mom, I didn't know you had a gun collection."

• Five-year-old Mark couldn't wait to tell his father about the movie he had watched on television, *20,000 Leagues Under the Sea.* The scenes with the submarine and the giant octopus had kept him wide-eyed. In the middle of the telling, Dad asked Mark, "What caused the submarine to sink?"

With a look of incredulity Mark replied, "Dad, it was the 20,000 leaks!"

A librarian in Powell, Wyoming, writes me:

> *A young boy, about six or seven years old, came into the library last week and asked my help to find a puppy-training video. We located an appropriate video for him, and he told us about his new beagle puppy. These videos check out for a week, so I was surprised the next day when the boy brought back the video and checked out a cartoon instead.*
>
> *While checking out the new video for him, I asked him, "How did that puppy-training video work for you?"*
>
> *"Oh, not very well," he replied. "I couldn't get him to watch it for long. At his age, he's mostly interested in food, you know."*

Children seem to possess a special affinity for generating bloopers about our fellow creatures that run and fly and hop and swim and crawl across our planet:

• A three-year-old boy went with his dad to see a litter of kittens. On returning home, he breathlessly informed his mother, "There were two boy kittens and two girl kittens."

"How did you know?" his mother asked.

"Daddy picked them up and looked underneath," he replied. "I think it's printed on the bottom."

• A group of young children were sitting in a circle with their teacher. She was going around in turn asking them all questions.

"Davy, what noise does a cow make?"

"It goes moo, miss."

"Alice, what noise does a cat make?"

"It goes meow, miss."

"Jamie, what sound does a lamb make?"

"It goes baa, miss."

"Jennifer, what sound does a mouse make?"

"Er . . . , it goes . . . click!"

• It was little Michael's first visit to the country, and feeding the chickens fascinated him. Early one morning he caught his first glimpse of a peacock strutting in the yard. Rushing indoors excitedly, Michael sought out his grandmother. "Oh, Granny," he exclaimed, "one of the chickens is in bloom!"

• The aunt of a four-year-old boy was pregnant and getting larger by the day. It just so happened that she had a cat who was pregnant too and who delivered her new litter one day.

A few days later, he patted his aunt's stomach and said to the entire family, "Know what's in here? KITTENS!!!"

• Little Billy entered the family vacation cabin with his grandfather. To keep from attracting pesky insects, they did not turn on the lights. Still, a few fireflies followed them in. Noticing the fireflies first, Billy whispered, "It's no use, Grandpa. The mosquitoes are coming after us with flashlights."

• As the weather grew cooler, Grandmother reminded her four-year-old granddaughter, Talia, "Close the door. There's a cold draft coming in."

Talia got a strange look on her face. A little apprehensive, but amazed and curious, she ran to the door and looked this way and that. Then, still curious but a little disappointed she turned to her grandmother and asked, "Where's the cold giraffe?"

• A ten-year-old girl asked and received help from a librarian on how to use the card catalog. In a little while the girl approached the librarian again, wanting to know how to spell "tequila."

"T-e-q-u-i-l-a," spelled the librarian, and the girl thanked her and went back to her search. A short time later she came to the desk, looking quite distraught.

"I just can't find it," she said.

"What book are you looking for, honey?" the librarian asked.

Replied the little girl, *"Tequila Mockingbird."*

THE KIDDISMS HALL OF FAME

- A mother was telling her little girl what her childhood was like: "We used to skate outside on a pond. I had a swing made from a tire. It hung from a tree in our front yard. We rode our pony. We picked wild raspberries in the woods."

  The little girl was wide-eyed taking this all in. At last she said, "I wish I had gotten to know you sooner!"

- Grandma decided to find out if her granddaughter had learned her colors yet. She pointed out object after object and asked the child what color each one was. The little girl answered each challenge correctly.

  Grandma was having so much fun that she continued. Finally, the child headed for the door, and, pursing her lips, she said, "Grandma, I think you should try to figure out some of these yourself!"

- A mother took her four-year-old son to a friend's birthday party, where the father of the birthday boy had rented a cotton-candy machine for the day. The visiting child refused to try any of the cotton candy and whimpered, "Mommy, you shouldn't eat insulation!"

"The k is silent!"

Classy Kiddisms

Real teachers drive old beater cars for which they can barely make the payments and whose insurance they can barely afford. Real teachers have lots of vacation time but no money to travel. Real teachers have stiff necks from writing on the blackboard while keeping their eyes on their students.

Real teachers possess incredible bladder capacity. Real teachers learn to inhale their lunch in as little as three minutes. Real teachers grade papers during commercials, in faculty meetings, in the car, in the bathroom, and at social and athletic events. Real teachers get paid to work six hours a day but actually work eight or more. Real teachers have no life at the end of a semester and very little the rest of the school year.

Real teachers have their best conferences in parking lots. Real teachers know they can't reach all their students, but that doesn't stop them from trying. Real teachers are some of the bravest, most altruistic, and most underpaid people you've ever met.

And real teachers chuckle at the kiddisms they receive from their beloved pupils:

• A first-grade teacher was reading the story of The Three Little Pigs to her class. She came to the part, where the first pig was trying to accumulate the building materials for his home: "And so the pig went up to the man with the wheelbarrow full of straw and said, 'Pardon me, sir, but may I have some of that straw to build my house?'"

The teacher paused then asked the class, "And what do you think that man said?"

One little boy raised his hand and opined, "I think he said, 'Wow! A talking pig!'"

• The kindergarten teacher asked her students what color they would get if they mixed blue and yellow. A little boy immediately shouted, "Green!" The teacher, impressed with the quick response, asked the boy how he knew.

"My mommy puts this blue stuff in the potty, and when I do a pee, it turns green."

• The children had all been photographed, and the teacher was trying to persuade each of them to buy a copy of the group picture. "Just think how nice it will be to look at it when you are all grown up and say, 'There's Jennifer; she's a lawyer,' or 'That's Michael. He's a doctor.'"

A small voice at the back of the room rang out, "And there's the teacher. She's dead."

• A fourth-grade teacher was giving her pupils a lesson in logic. "Here is the situation," she said. "A man is standing up in a boat in the middle of a river, fishing. He loses his balance, falls in, and begins splashing and yelling for help. His wife hears the commotion, knows he can't swim, and runs down to the bank. Why do you think she ran to the bank?"

A little girl raised her hand and asked, "To draw out all his savings?"

• Finding one of her students making faces at others on the playground, Ms. Smith stopped to gently reprove the child. Smiling sweetly, the Sunday school teacher said, "Bobby, when I was a child, I was told that if I made an ugly face, it would freeze and I would stay like that." Bobby looked up and replied, "Well, Ms. Smith, you can't say you weren't warned."

• The sixth-grade music class had just started when one student asked the teacher, "Are we going to sing with musical accompaniment today, or Acapulco?"

• Justin had worn glasses since the age of three. When he was in the first grade, he came home one day very distressed. Wanting to find out what was the matter, his mother asked, "Justin, what happened today to upset you so much?"

He answered, "It's not fair—I'm not allowed to go to the library."

His mother became very concerned and asked, "Why aren't you allowed to go to the library?"

Tearfully he replied, "Because in order to go to the library, you have to have supervision, and I wear glasses!"

• The new librarian decided that instead of checking out children's books by writing the names of borrowers on the book cards herself, she would have the youngsters sign their own names. She would then tell them they were signing a contract for returning the books on time.

Her first customer was a second-grader, who looked surprised to see a new librarian. He brought four books to the desk and shoved them across to her, giving her his name as he did so. The librarian pushed the books back and told him to sign them out.

The boy laboriously printed his name on each book card and then handed them to her and said, "You're different."

When the librarian asked how she was different, the boy said, "That other librarian we had could write."

• Ray's preschool class went on a field trip to the fire station. The firefighter giving the presentation held up a smoke detector and asked the class: "Does anyone know what this is?"

Ray's hand shot up, and the firefighter called on him. "That's how Mommy knows supper is ready!"

• When Frank was in sixth grade he took peanut-butter-and-jelly sandwiches to school every day. His mother finally asked him if he was sick of them. He replied, "Heck no. They're the best kind for trading."

• While taking a routine vandalism report at an elementary school, a policewoman was interrupted by a little girl about six years old. Looking up and down at the policewoman's uniform, she asked, "Are you a cop?"

"Yes," answered the policewoman and continued writing the report.

"My mother said if I ever needed help, I should ask the police. Is that right?"

"Yes, that's right."

"Well, then, would you please tie my shoe?"

• Sarah's school held a "drug free" parade and rally, with speakers encouraging the kids to keep away from drugs and to stay in school. When the six-year-old came home from school, her mother asked her what she learned about drugs that day. Sarah replied, "Drugs are free at my school!"

• A little girl in first grade was doing very well, especially in spelling. One day she came home with new words to study for an upcoming test, and she asked her mother to help. They came to the word "knit," and her mother asked her to spell it.

She said, "N-i-t."

Her mother said, "No, try again."

She said, very slowly, "N-i-t."

Her mother said, "Now, honey, I know you know how to spell this word. Try again."

Aggravated, she spelled very slowly, as if her mother was just not getting the whole picture, "N-I-T!"

Finally, her mother told her that the correct spelling was *k-n-i-t*. The little girl looked at her mother, put her hands on her hips, and said, "The *k* is silent!"

• When Maria, the daughter of William Howard Taft III, was a shy schoolgirl, her teacher asked her for a brief family history. This is what Maria wrote: "My great-grandfather was president of the United States. My grandfather was senator from Ohio. My father is ambassador to Ireland. I am a Brownie."

I spent a terrific day working with fourth- and fifth-graders at Adobe Bluffs Elementary School in Penasquitos, California, as a visiting lecturer about language fun. Kids that age are bundles of hormones poured into sneakers, but they respond enthusiastically to puns, palindromes, and other kinds of language fun. In fact, the children made posters to celebrate my coming, and these placards included "Richard Lederer, the Famous Writer" and "Richard Lederer, the Popular Speaker."

But my favorite placard read "Richard Lederer, the Wanted Comedian."

THE CLASSROOM KIDDISMS
HALL OF FAME

- On the first day of school, the kindergarten teacher said, "If anyone has to go to the bathroom, hold up two fingers."

  Asked a little girl, "How will that help?"

- A fifth-grade teacher told her students that members of her profession in the 1800s dressed in ankle-length skirts and long-sleeve blouses, even in summertime. She went on to say that such garb was necessary because teachers were not allowed to expose their arms or legs.

  A boy piped up from the back of the classroom, "Oh no, that can't be true. The Constitution gave everyone the right to bare arms."

- Ms. Mayfield had been giving her second-grade pupils a lesson on science. She had explained magnets and shown how they could pick up nails and other bits of iron. Now it was question time, and she asked, "My name begins with the letter *M,* and I pick things up. What am I?"

  A little boy in the front row said, "You're a mother."

"Mommy can't come to the phone . . . right now. She's hitting the bottle."

Blessed Be
the Children

A Sunday School teacher began her lesson with a question: "Boys and girls, what do we know about God?"

A hand shot up in the air. "He is an artist!" said the kindergarten boy.

"Really? How do you know?" the teacher asked.

"You know—Our Father, who does art in Heaven . . ."

From these kinds of slips of the ear, we can construct a Lord's Prayer composed entirely of kiddisms:

Our Father, Art, in heaven, Harold be thy name.
Thy king done come. Thy will be done,
On earth as it is in heaven.
Give us this day our jelly bread
And forgive us our trash passes
As we forgive those who pass trash against us.
And lead us not into Penn Station,
But deliver us some e-mail. . . .

There's something about kids and religion that has sparked forth some of the most charming kiddisms in my collection:

• A Sunday school teacher was observing her classroom of children while they drew. She would occasionally walk around to see each child's artwork. As she got to one little girl who was working diligently, she asked what the drawing was. The girl replied, "I'm drawing God."

The teacher paused and said, "But no one knows what God looks like."

Without missing a beat or looking up from her drawing, the girl replied, "They will in a minute."

• *A little boy's prayer:* "Dear God, please take care of my daddy and my mommy and my sister and my brother and my doggy and me. Oh, please take care of yourself, God. If anything happens to you, we're gonna be in a big mess."

• A teacher was explaining the story of Noah and his ark to her young students. She asked the class if they thought Noah did a lot of fishing during the flood.

"No," said a bright boy, "he had only two worms."

• When three-year-old Kelli would finish her nightly prayers, she would always say, "All girls."

One evening, Mother asked her, "Kelli, why do you always add the part about all girls?"

Her response: "Because we always finish our prayers by saying All Men!"

• A little girl stared questioningly at her grandfather. Finally she asked, "Grandpa, were you on Noah's Ark?"

The grandfather replied with a slight chuckle, "Of course not."

Then the girl asked, "Then how come you didn't drown?"

• A pupil in Bible class confidently recited the names of the five books of Moses: "Genesis, Exodus, Lexus . . ."

• A teacher was testing her Sunday school class to see if they understood the concept of getting to Heaven.

She asked them, "If I sold my house and my car, had a big garage sale, and gave all my money to the Church, would that get me into Heaven?"

"No!" the children answered.

"If I cleaned the church building every day, mowed the yard, and kept everything neat and tidy, would that get me into Heaven?"

Again, the answer was, "No!"

"Well, then, if I was kind to animals and gave candy to all the children, and loved my husband, would that get me into Heaven?"

Again, the class all answered, "No!"

The teacher was just bursting with pride for her pupils and continued, "Then how can I get into Heaven?"

A five-year-old boy shouted out, "You gotta be dead!"

• Little Bobby was spending the weekend with his grandmother after a particularly trying week in kindergarten. His grandmother decided to take him to the park on Saturday morning. It had been snowing all night, and everything was beautiful.

His grandmother remarked, "Doesn't it look like an artist painted this scenery? Did you know God painted this just for you?"

Bobby said, "Yes, God did it, and he did it left-handed."

This confused his grandmother a bit, and she asked him, "What makes you say God did this with his left hand?"

"Well," said Bobby, "we learned at Sunday School last week that Jesus sits on God's right hand!"

• After lunch one Sunday morning, a father asked his seven-year-old son, "What did you learn in Sunday School?"

The boy told him about the man who had fallen among thieves

and had been beaten and left helpless by the side of the road. None of the passersby stopped to offer help until finally one considerate man did stop and gave aid. The father asked his son if he knew who the helpful man was.

"Oh yes," he replied. "He was a good smart American."

• While walking along the sidewalk in front of his church, a minister heard the intoning of a prayer that nearly made his collar wilt. Apparently, his five-year-old son Michael and his playmates had found a dead robin. Feeling that proper burial should be performed, they had secured a small box and cotton batting, then dug a hole and made ready for the disposal of the deceased.

The minister's son was chosen to say the appropriate prayers and with sonorous dignity intoned his version of what he thought his father always said: "Glory be unto the Father and unto the Son, and into the hole he goes."

• A woman was trying hard to get the catsup to come out of the jar. During her struggle the phone rang, so she asked her four-year-old daughter to answer it. "It's the minister, Mommy," the child said to her mother. Then she added, "Mommy can't come to the phone to talk to you right now. She's hitting the bottle."

• It was that time during the Sunday morning service for the children's sermon, and all the children were invited to come forward. One little girl was wearing a particularly pretty dress, and as she sat down, the pastor leaned over and said to her, "That is a very pretty dress. Is it your Easter dress?"

The little girl replied, directly into the pastor's clip-on microphone, "Yes, and my Mom says it's a bitch to iron."

• A rabbi was giving a lesson to a group of children on the 23rd Psalm. He noticed that one of the little boys seemed disquieted by the sentence "surely, goodness and mercy will follow me all the days of my life."

"What's wrong with that, Gerald?" the rabbi asked.

"Well," answered Gerald, "I understand about having goodness and mercy, for God is good. But I'm not sure I'd like Shirley following me around all the time."

• A girl asked her new seven-year-old neighbor, "What church do you go to?"

"I don't go to church," her playmate said. "I go to a temple. I'm Jewish."

"What's that?" asked the first little girl.

"You know there are Protestants, Catholics, and Jews," the girl explained. "But they are all just different ways of voting for God."

• An eight-year-old returned from Sunday school and announced, "Today I learned about the first Jews. And their names were Abraham Lincoln and Sarah."

• A father was reading Bible stories to his young son: "The man named Lot was warned to take his wife and flee out of the city, but his wife looked back and was turned to salt."

His son asked, "What happened to the flea?"

• Nine-year-old Joey was asked by his mother what he had learned in Sunday School. "Well, Mom, our teacher told us how God sent Moses behind enemy lines on a rescue mission to lead the Israelites out of Egypt. When he got to the Red Sea, he had his engineers build a pontoon bridge, and all the people walked across safely. He used his walkie-talkie to radio headquarters and call in an air strike. They sent in bombers to blow up the bridge, and all the Israelites were saved."

"Now, Joey, is that *really* what your teacher taught you?" his mother asked.

"Well, no, Mom, but if I told it the way the teacher did, you'd never believe it!"

• A friend's grandson was reading with his granddad about Adam and Eve. He asked, "Is this where God took out the man's brain and made a woman?"

• Little Johnny and his family were having Sunday dinner at his grandmother's house. Everyone was seated around the table as the food was being served. When little Johnny received his plate, he started eating right away.

"Johnny, wait until we say our prayer."

"I don't have to," the boy replied.

"Of course you do," his mother insisted. "We say a prayer before eating at our house."

"That's our house," Johnny explained. "But this is grandma's house, and *she* knows how to cook!"

• At Sunday School they were teaching how God created everything, including human beings. Little Johnny seemed especially intent when they told him how Eve was created out of one of Adam's ribs. Later in the week, his mother noticed him lying down as though he were ill. She said, "Johnny what is the matter?"

Little Johnny responded, "I have a pain in my side. I think I'm going to have a wife."

• After a church service one Sunday morning, a young boy suddenly announced to his mother, "Mom, I've decided to become a minister when I grow up."

"That's okay with us, but what made you decide that?"

"Well," said the little boy, "I have to go to church on Sunday anyway, and I figure it will be more fun to stand up and yell, than to sit down and listen."

• A little girl became restless as the preacher's sermon dragged on and on. Finally, she leaned over to her mother and whispered, "Mommy, if we give him the money now, will he let us go?"

• A Sunday school teacher recited to her class the story of Jesus and the ten lepers. "Children, what do we call people who have leprosy?" she asked.

Little five-year-old Alex enthusiastically shouted out, "Leprechauns!"

• A minister went to an informal church gathering, wearing shorts and a T-shirt. A little girl who had seen him only in his Sunday morning suits loudly called out, "Hey, Pastor, you sure look different with clothes on!"

• A little girl was sitting on her grandfather's lap as he read her a bedtime story. From time to time, she would take her eyes off the book and reach up to touch his wrinkled cheek.

She asked, "Grandpa, did God make you?"

"Yes, sweetheart," he answered. "God made me a long time ago."

"Oh," she paused. "Grandpa, did God make me, too?"

"Yes, indeed, honey," he said. "God made you just a little while ago."

"God's getting better at it, isn't He?"

THE SUNDAY SCHOOL BLOOPERS HALL OF FAME

- The Bible is full of many interesting caricatures. Michael Angelo painted them on the Sixteen Chapels.
- Samson slayed the Philistines with the axe of the apostles. He slayed them by pulling down the pillows of the temple.
- Moses went up on Mount Cyanide to get the Ten Amendments. The First Commandment was when Eve told Adam to eat the apple. The Fifth Commandment is humor they father and thy mother. The Ninth Commandment is thou shalt not bare faults witness. And the Tenth Commandment is thou shalt not take the covers off thy neighbor's wife.
- When the three wise guys from the East Side arrived, they found Jesus in the manager rapped in waddling clothes.

The author of The Communist Manifesto *was Harpo Marx.*

Super-duper Student Bloopers

A kindergartner came home from her first day at school, and her mother asked her, "What did you learn in school today?"

"Not enough," replied the little girl. "They say I have to go back tomorrow."

And back to school do students go—day after day and year after year.

One of the great pleasures of being a teacher is facilitating and observing that delightful, wondrous process by which children learn to successfully navigate the tricky tributaries, slippery streams, and fickle fjords of the ever-fluid English language. While serving as river guides to young scholars necessarily means wading through lots of soggy syntax, teachers take comfort in knowing that before too long their students will be on solid ground. There, hopefully, they will no longer be satisfied to write, as students actually did, that "the Greeks invented three kinds of columns—Corinthian, Ironic, and Dorc," or that "Sir Francis Drake circumcised the world with a 100-foot clipper."

Sooner or later, the young scholars who wrote, "In 1957, Eugene O'Neill won a Pullet Surprise" and "Romeo's last wish was to be laid by Juliet" will know better. And they'll be richer for the knowledge, of course.

Their teachers, however, will be just a little poorer for it—or would be, if there wasn't always a new crop of kids right behind the last, ever ready, like their predecessors, to roll up their sleeves, dip into their wellspring of words, and pull out sentences that, while technically wrong, somehow manage to seem so very, very . . . write on.

Here's a sampling of the kind of English terrors and tinglish errors, the blood and thunder and thud and blunder, that keep teachers laughing—and crying. We were all students, so who among us does not have empathy for the creators of schoolish bloopers? Thus, I present them for your enjoyment, not your ridicule:

• No sooner had the Hebrews left the Mess in Potamia safely behind them than they found themselves caught in the Fatal Crescent.

• Pharos, the Egyptian king, decried that the Hebrews should be drafted into farced labor building the Pyrenees and that if any of them bulked, they should be put into stocks and bonds.

• The gift that the Phoenicians gave to civilization was Phoenician blinds.

• Grease was on the rise.

• All Gaul is quartered unto three halves.

• In ancient Rome, women had a high risk of childbirth.

• The four gospels were written by John, Paul, George, and that other guy.

- Beowulf was an epic worrier.
- In Walter Scott's book, the Knight Templar wanted Rebecca to submit to him, but she reclined to do so.
- Joan of Arc is a true mortar and a true heroine.
- Don Quixote tried to tip the windmill.
- Oliver Cromwell had a large red nose, but under it were deeply religious feelings.
- The earl of Sandwich was the first man to put his meat between two slices of bread.
- The ship that brought the first settlers to the new world was the *Cauliflower*.
- Martha Stewart sewed the first American flag.
- One of the problems faced by President Jefferson was the Cheapskate Affair.
- Pennsylvania was settled by the Pennsylvania Douch.
- Edgar Allan Poe's single-effect theory is that everything in the story contributes to one main idea and that the story should be short enough to be read in a single shitting.
- The election of President Lincoln caused the South to recede.
- Harriet Beecher Stowe wrote *Uncle Ben's Cabin*.
- An Indian woman squatted over a fire in one teepee, and you could smell fresh meat cooking.
- Philip Buster was a prominent American.
- The author of *The Communist Manifesto* was Harpo Marx.
- A landmark in Paris is the Eyeful Tower.
- Art Deco built a lot of buildings in Chicago.
- The president is elected by the electrical college.
- The legislature makes the laws, the executive carries them out, and the judiciary interrupts them.
- Checks and balances: When an official checks the books and they balance.
- Someone who runs for an office he already holds is called an incompetent.
- One argument against capital punishment is that the prisoner will have a grudge against society.

- While he may be poor and shabby, underneath those ragged trousers beats a heart of gold.
- My arms are slender, with just enough hair on them to be unnoticeable.
- There are more dead people than living, and their numbers are increasing.
- A class of high-school students was especially talkative one day, and their teacher had had enough. "All right!" he shouted. "The next person who talks is going to be severely castigated!"

The class immediately went quiet, until one of the students asked, "How are you going to do that to a girl?"
- The creative writing teacher instructed her young students to describe in their papers what was really inside them. One of the compositions handed in contained this sentence: "In me there is my stomach, my liver, my lungs, three cookies, and a peanut-butter-and-jelly sandwich."

THE HALL OF FAME
OF HISTORY BLOOPERS

- The inhabitants of ancient Egypt were called mummies, and they all wrote in hydraulics.
- Julius Caesar extinguished himself on the battlefields of Gaul. The Ides of March murdered him because they thought he was going to be made king. Caesar expired with these immortal words upon his dying lips: "Eat you, Brutus!"
- Christopher Columbus discovered America while cursing about the Atlantic on the *Nina,* the *Pintacolada,* and the *Santa Fe.*
- Abraham Lincoln became America's greatest Precedent. Lincoln's mother died in infancy, and he was born in a log cabin which he built with his very own hands. When Lincoln was president, he wore only a tall silk hat. He said, "In onion there is strength." Abraham Lincoln wrote the Gettysburg Address while traveling from Washington to Gettysburg on the back of an envelope.
- Martin Luther had a dream. He went to Washington and recited his "Sermon on the Monument." Later, he nailed 96 Protestants in the Watergate Scandal, which ushered in a new error in the anals of human history.

Elephants eat roots, leaves, grasses, and sometimes bark.

Science Fantasies

It sometimes happens that the genesis of an important scientific discovery has less to do with rigorously applied laboratory methodology than it does with a serendipitous accident. Penicillin, X rays, Newton's theory of gravitation, Pasteur's principle of vaccination, the big bang theory, the discovery of DNA, safety glass, Teflon, Velcro, Post-It notes—all resulted in large part from happenstance intersecting with informed, creative intuition. Scientists have dubbed this phenomenon "the Principle of Limited Sloppiness." Parents are advised to stave off as long as possible their children's awareness of this legitimate scientific theory. It could counter an explanation being made for why a child's room looks like the result of an explosion.

It's easy enough to say that the following statements, taken from exams, lab reports, essays, and oral presentations given by scientist students, are, well, a tad sloppy. But each also proves the point that every so often, through no intention whatsoever, one ends up with something that in its own way is better than—or at least as much fun as—whatever one had started out meaning to produce in the first place:

- Copernicus's theory claimed that the Sun was on the center of the earth.
- Gravity is a pulling type thing that makes sure that the planets don't fall or hurt anything.
- When a planet first forms, it is like a big ball of mucus.
- The Sun is a red giant that will be replaced by another red giant before the giant fussies out and dies.
- Gas giants suffer from equatorial bulge.
- Black holes are formed by unknown matters of solids as well as the gases, which contain hydrogen, helium, carbon, etc. If you were in a black hole, your head would be at your feet.
- Before Galileo, no one could see the Moon.
- Some oxygen molecules help fires burn while others help make water, so sometimes it's brother against brother.
- A vibration is a motion that cannot make up its mind which way it wants to go.
- *Australopithecus* was first found by leaking in Olduvai Gorge.
- Salk perfected the Salk vaccine, an anecdote for polo.
- To most people solutions mean finding the answers. But to chemists solutions are things that are still all mixed up.
- When they broke open molecules, they found they were stuffed with atoms. But when they broke open atoms, they found them stuffed with explosions.
- In looking at a drop of water under a microscope, we find there are twice as many Hs as Os.

- Darwin's book stated that all animals evolved from primeval man.
- I am fascinated by the invisible world of microorgasms.
- Dinosaurs used to smell bad, but they don't anymore because they are extinct.
- Given their massive size, dinosaurs must have been fearful creatures.
- Elephants eat roots, leaves, grasses, and sometimes bark.
- Spiders freeze in winter and unthaw in spring.
- An animal or plant species can also be described as the kind of animal and plant species that it is.
- It's in a state of animated suspension.
- A spine is the long bone that goes down your back. Your head sits on one end, and you sit on the other.
- Cyanide is so poisonous that one drop of it on a dog's tongue will kill the strongest man.
- Isotherms and isobars are even more important than their names sound.
- It is so hot in some places that the people there have to live in other places.
- A fibula is a small lie.
- A disease associated with smoking is premature death.
- When you get old, so do your bowels, and you get intercontinental.
- Some viruses can lie doormat for years.
- Food is taken into the mouth and masturbated.
- When a boy reaches puberty, he says good-bye to his boyhood and looks forward to his adultery.
- Many young girls are getting pregnant every day.
- I feel that if you are going to have sex with your boyfriend or husband, you should use some kind of conception.
- With the naked eye, you can only observe what you see.

Meteorology is another scientific discipline fraught with science friction:

Ralph was absent yesterday because he had a sore trout.

That's No Excuse

A perpetual lack of power is the bane of every child's life. If Mom or Dad says you're going to the dentist, you'll be squirming in a waiting room chair in less time than it takes to pull you out from beneath your bed.

If your parents forbid you to watch TV, you'll stare into that empty, gray screen until you simply give up trying to get anyone to notice you, much less feel sorry for you.

If broccoli is on that night's menu, no amount of wishing will turn it into candy corn.

In the world of Parents versus Kids, parents win, every time.

- Clouds are high-flying fogs. I am not sure how clouds get formed. But the clouds know how to do it, and that is the important thing. Clouds just keep circling the earth around and around. And around. There is not much else to do.
- Humidity is the experience of looking for air and finding water. We keep track of the humidity in the air so we won't drown when we breathe.
- Rain is saved up in cloud banks. It is often known as soft water and oppositely known as hail.
- A blizzard is when it snows sideways.
- A hurricane is a breeze of a bigly size.
- The wind is like the air, only pushier.
- A monsoon is a French gentleman.

Lest you think that science friction is limited to students, consider this recent statement by a purportedly grown-up reporter: "Wednesday, August 27, Mars will be making its closest approach to Earth. Go outside and look at Mars tonight. We won't be seeing it again for 248 years."

THE UNSCIENTIFIC HALL OF FAME

- Iron was first smelled in 1759.
- The four stages of metamorphosis are egg, lava, pupil, adult.
- A molecule is so small that it can't be seen by the naked observer.
- A fossil is an extinct animal. The older it is, the more extinct it gets.
- The equator is an imaginary lion that runs around the world forever.
- Heredity means that if your grandfather didn't have any children, then your father probably wouldn't have any, and neither would you, probably.

Except when it comes to the excuse note. Here, finally, is a means by which children have transferred unto themselves the full (or, we might say, the unadulterated) power of one grown-up over another. What child, walking to school with a parent's excuse note firmly in pocket, isn't heartened by the knowledge that, even if nothing else good happens that day, at least they'll get to hand in one paper with which their teacher is guaranteed not to have a problem.

It's probably best that most of us were not inclined to scrutinize our parents' excuse notes too carefully. As we're about to see, doing so might have seriously compromised our sense of indomitability. On the other hand, it might also have given us some insight into why, when we watched our teachers reading those notes, we sometimes saw a most peculiar expression come over their faces.

Imagine trying to maintain a teacher's air of dignified authority while reading any of the following all-too-real excuse notes:

- Please excuse Raul from school yesterday. He had a stomach egg.
- Susan was not in school today because she had her first menopause.
- Stanley had to miss some school. He had an attack of whooping cranes in his chest.
- Gerald was out last week because his grandmother died in Kentucky again.
- Please excuse Margie for being absent Wednesday and Thursday as she was sick with a stripped throat and an absent tooth.
- Ralph was absent yesterday because he had a sore trout.
- Please refuse Robert's absents last Friday. He had a sour thought.
- Ronnie could not finish his work last night. He said his brain was too tired of spelling.
- Please excuse Stanley. The basement of our house got flooded where the children sleep so they had to be evaporated.
- I kept Monica home today because she was not feeling too bright.

- Please excuse my daughter. She had an abominable pain.
- Please can Jill not have Jim today? She had Jim last week and is still sore.
- Please excuse Lupe. She is having problems with her ovals.
- Please forgive Clarence for being absent from school the past few days. He was home sick from an operation. He had trouble and had to be serpent sized.
- Please excuse Redbird. Every time she coff she make whoopie.
- Jennifer was late due to our clock getting unplugged and waking up late.
- Please excuse the stink on Bill's clothes. We've been spraying the garden because it is full of abnoxous incests.
- Please excuse Jane. She had an absent tooth. Wednesday she will have an appointment with the ornithologist.
- Please excuse my daughter's absence for the past week, as she had a case of the fool.
- Please excuse my daughter's absence. She had her periodicals.
- Please excuse Connie from gym class to day, as she had difficulty breeding.
- Paulie was late because he was not too early. He is never in no hurry. He is too slow to be quick.

Is there any excuse for the disrepair of these excuse notes? Or are the parents just too slow to be quick?

THE EXCUSES, EXCUSES HALL OF FAME

- My son is under the doctor's care. Please execute him.
- Please excuse Mary for being absent. She was sick, and I had her shot.
- Please excuse Jimmy for being. It was his father's fault.
- Please excuse Tom for being absent yesterday. He had diarrhea, and his boots leak.
- Maryann was absent December 11–16 because she had a fever, sore throat, headache, and upset stomach. Her sister was also sick—fever and sore throat—and her brother had a low-grade fever and ached all over. I wasn't the best either—sore throat and fever. There must be the flu going around school. Her father even got hot last night.

The Gift of Gaffes

"My vision is to make the most diverse state on earth, and we have people from every planet...on the earth in this state.
—Gray Davis, former governor of California

Playing Politics

Why is it that the statement "that kid could definitely grow up to be a politician" raises eyebrows and paints smirks on the faces of those who hear it?

Aren't politicians, after all, the very lifeblood of our democracy? Don't we free citizens, alone inside the voting booth, quietly and optimistically entrust our politicians with some of our brightest dreams, our deep-down belief that good men and women, working together, really can make each day better than the last?

Don't politicians offer us the means of realizing our cherished hopes for the future? Isn't what makes them special the fact that they *want* to play that role in the life of the body politic—that they are men and women so moved by the idea and ideals of public service that they choose to dedicate their lives to working for the good of all of us, rather than for their own personal gain or benefit?

Isn't every American politician, in fact, doing nothing less than holding high the torch first lit—nay, first *conceived!*—by the glorious, trailblazing, world-altering genius of our Founding Fathers and Mothers?

You betcha.

So why, then, is it almost impossible to take politicians seriously?

While we ponder that mystery, let us take a moment to reflect upon what a few of them have recently had to say:

Along with the rest of the country, I have been amused and amazed by our president's Bushisms. The term *Bushism* was actually coined from the tongue tangles of Dubya's father, George Herbert Walker Bush, a pioneering master of language run a-mock:

• For seven-and-a-half years I've worked alongside President Reagan. We've had triumphs. Made some mistakes. We've had some sex . . . ugh . . . setbacks.

• I want to make sure everybody who has a job wants a job.

• It's no exaggeration to say that the undecideds could go one way or another.

• I have opinions of my own—strong opinions—but I don't always agree with them.

But President George W. Bush's fractured English has outslipped his father's:

• I know how hard it is to put food on your family.

• Will the highways on the Internet become more few?

• We cannot let terrorists and rogue nations hold this nation hostile or hold our allies hostile.

• The senator has got to understand if he's going to have—he can't have it both ways. He can't take the high horse and then claim the low road.

• I am mindful not only of preserving executive powers for myself, but for my predecessors as well.

• Quite frankly, teachers are the only profession that teach our children.

• For every fatal shooting, there were roughly three nonfatal shootings. And, folks, this is unacceptable in America. It's just unacceptable. And we're going to do something about it.

A politician was rousingly introduced with these deathless words: "He is a man whose life is patterned on firm, moral principles, and believe me, there are very few of those left!" When it comes to politics, we have to wonder if there are any logic and sense of style left:

• When a great many people are unable to find work, unemployment results.

—*President Calvin Coolidge*

• Things are more like they are now than they have ever been.

—*President Gerald Ford*

• As many of you know, I was very instrumental in the founding of the Internet.

—*Al Gore, vice president and presidential candidate*

• I actually did vote for the $87 billion, before I voted against it.

—*presidential candidate John Kerry, on voting against
a military funding bill for U.S. troops in Iraq*

Vice President Dan Quayle was so (in)famous for his muffs of the mouth that they spawned a newsletter that chronicled his Quaylisms:

• Mars is essentially in the same orbit. Mars is somewhat the same distance from the Sun, which is very important. We have seen pictures where there are canals, we believe, and water. If there is water, that means there is oxygen. If oxygen, that means we can breathe.

• What a waste it is to lose one's mind—or not to have a mind. How true that is.

• I believe we are on an irreversible trend toward more freedom and democracy. But that could change.

• If we don't succeed, we run the risk of failure.

As far as clear thinking goes, no one can beat Secretary of Defense Donald Rumsfeld, who was a champion college wrestler. Here is Rumsfeld, wrestling with an attempt at logic: "There are known knowns. These are things that we know we know. There are known unknowns. That is to say, there are things that we know we don't know. But there are also unknown unknowns, the ones we don't know we don't know."

The following poli-tickles are guaranteed to tickle the body politic and demonstrate that the term *political science* is an oxymoron:

• I think that gay marriage is something that should be between a man and a woman.

—*California governor Arnold Schwarzenegger*

• My vision is to make the most diverse state on earth, and we have people from every planet... on the earth in this state.

—*Gray Davis, the California governor whom Arnold replaced*

• Nixon has been sitting in the White House while George McGovern has been exposing himself to the people of the United States.

—*Rhode Island governor Frank Licht, campaigning for McGovern in 1972*

• Whadaya mean nepotism? He's my brother!

—*Philadelphia mayor Frank Rizzo, when asked if his appointing his brother as fire commissioner constituted nepotism*

- I am a great mayor; I am an upstanding Christian man; I am an intelligent man. I am a deeply educated man. I am a humble man.

—*Marion Barry, mayor of Washington, D.C.*

- I want to thank you from the bottom of my heart and from my wife's bottom, too.

—*the mayor of Montreal*

- Our communities need a partner in crime, and that partner should be the city government.

—*El Paso, Texas, political ad*

- We've been trying to get the dog ordinance down on paper for years.

—*a San Diego councilman*

- I am adamantly opposed to forcing anyone to undergo voluntary sterilization.

—*another councilman*

- This is the worst disaster in California since I was elected.

—*California governor Pat Brown, discussing a local flood*

"If you open that Pandora's box, you never know what Trojan horses will jump out," famously observed Ernest Bevin, Britain's postwar foreign secretary. Mixed-up logic inevitably leads to mixed-up metaphors:

- No one wants to say the sky is falling, but in this instance I am afraid the emperor has no clothes. Despite Herculean efforts by the council and council staff, we are still only dealing with the tip of the iceberg.

- We are in a butt-ugly recession right now, but we are seeing enough light at the end of the tunnel.
- If this thing starts to snowball, it will catch fire right across the country.
- We have derailed the ship of state.
- We are being inundated by an avalanche of creeping paralysis.

Political tickles also dance on the tongues of the people who cover the tough-and-rumble, thud-and-blunder arena of politics. A news bite just before a commercial break informed the listeners that "Senator Ted Kennedy said that the cost of the Medicare program would be about one billion dollars. More in a minute." This had most of the state of Michigan laughing for two days and quite embarrassed the news anchor, who will likely think next time before extemporizing on the air.

THE HALL OF FAME OF POLI-TICKLES

- No sane person in the country likes the war in Viet Nam, and neither does President Johnson.

  —Vice President Hubert H. Humphrey

- Capital punishment is our society's recognition of the sanctity of human life.

  —Utah senator Orrin Hatch

- I am privileged to speak at this millstone in the history of Dartmouth College.

  —New Hampshire governor John King

- I didn't say that I didn't say it. I said that I didn't say that I said it. I want to make that very clear.

  —Michigan governor George Romney

- The West Virginia legislature passed a law forbidding "picking flora and fauna within a hundred yards of a highway."

They'll be watching Mike Tyson with a fine-tooth comb from now on.

Making Sport of English

The great Washington Redskins quarterback Joe Theismann once said, "Nobody in the game of football should be called a genius. A genius is somebody like Norman Einstein."

Now, what are we to make of Mr. Theismann's observation? Ever the champion, he may have been making his bid to become, however fleetingly, the funniest man alive. More likely, of course, it was simply a slip of the tongue.

Yogi Berra, the legendary Yankees catcher, taped a Visa commercial with Houston Rockets center Yao Ming. While visiting the Fox broadcast booth, Yogi talked about how much he had enjoyed working with the seven-and-a half-foot Yao, but added, "The only problem was that he don't speak English too good."

Athletes dazzle us with their skill on the field and court and in the arena and ring. But sometimes they don't speak English too good. There does seem to be something about sports that invites linguistic fumbles, balks, and air balls. If, as singer-songwriter Elvis Costello once asserted, "Writing about music is like dancing about architecture," then perhaps talking about sports is like ice-skating about medicine or yodeling about math. Perhaps they just don't go together:

- If I'd have hit that harder, I'd of missed it closer.

  —Yogi Berra, while playing in a golf tournament

- I was big, even when I was little.

  —Chicago Bears' lineman William, "Refrigerator" Perry,
  who reached 400 pounds

- It's a once-in-a-lifetime thing that only happens every so often.

  —Minnesota Vikings wide receiver Randy Moss, on his no-look
  lateral to a teammate for a touchdown

- We've been working on the basics because, basically, we've been having trouble with the basics.

  —Bob Ojeda, baseball pitcher

- Nobody wants to be in my pants right now.

  —Juan Rincone, Minnesota Twins pitcher
  after getting shelled by the Yankees

- I have two weapons—my legs, my arm, and my brains.

  —Atlanta Falcons star quarterback Michael Vick,
  on the secret of his success

- I owe a lot to my parents, especially my mother and father.

  —golfer Greg Norman

- Let's let bye-byes be bye-byes.

  —baseball star Ricky Henderson, burying the hatchet with
  Lou Pinella

- I just might fade into Bolivian. I don't know where to go, what to do.

  —Mike Tyson, after being thrashed by Lennox Lewis

- I didn't know Elvis was from Memphis. I thought he was from Tennessee.

  —Memphis Grizzlies player Drew Gooden, when asked about
  visiting Graceland

- When it rains, it snows.

  —Tampa Bay Buccaneer free safety Dexter Jackson,
  after a lopsided loss

- If they did, I don't remember it.

  —Boston Red Sox outfielder Manny Ramirez, when asked if his
  team had tested him for attention deficit disorder

- I'm playing as well as I've ever played, except for the years I played better.

  —Fred Couples on his golf game

- It's not going to be peaches and gravy all the time.

  —Indiana Pacers center Brad Miller during a team slump

- This isn't going to be a walk in the cake.

  —Philadelphia 76ers center Dikembe Mutombo on the prospect of playing the Los Angeles Lakers in the finals

- I don't have the first clue who he is talking about, because all I worry about is Jerome.

  —Seattle SuperSonics center Jerome James, responding to charges by his coach that he was a selfish player

Managers and coaches don't fare any better than their players:

- The only reason we're 7-0 is because we've won all seven of our games.

  —David Garcia

- Our strength is that we don't have any weaknesses. Our weakness is that we don't have any real strengths.

  —Frank Broyles

- After all, where would our team be without their supporters?

  —Hank Stram

- Men, I want you just thinking of one word all season. One word and one word only: Super Bowl.

  —Bill Peterson

- Not only is he ambidextrous, but he can throw with either hand.

  —Duffy Daugherty

- I have nothing to say, and I'll only say it once.

  —Floyd Smith

- That's the Italian city with the guys in the boats, right?

  —boxing promoter Murad Muhammad on the possibility of
  staging a fight in Venezuela

In television, you talk until you can think of something to say, observed University of South Carolina football coach Lou Holtz on his days as a network analyst. Holtz's conclusion is apparently true about broadcasters:

- Anytime Detroit scores more than 100 points and holds the other team below 100 points, they almost always win.

  —Doug Collins

- I'm not sure what his points are, but without knowing what his points are, I'd say he has some good points.

  —tennis star and commentator John McEnroe on the comments
  of another player

- That's one of the best sets I've ever seen Tomas Zib play—although I should preface that by saying I haven't seen him play before.

  —John McEnroe

- If Pete Rose brings the Reds in, they ought to bronze him and put him in cement.

  —Harry Caray

- Tony Gwynn has been named player of the year for April.

  —Ralph Kiner

• Leo Label has been competing with a pulled stomach muscle, showing a lot of guts.

—Jim McKay

• Vasquez is throwing up on the bull pen.

—Jerry Coleman

• He ran so hard he was left grasping for air.

—Keith Jackson

• The 78-yard drive was led by 14-year-old veteran Lenny Dawson.

—Curt Gowdy

• A bunch of epitaphs are coming out of the mouth of John Rocker.

—José Vargas

• This is Gregoriava from Bulgaria. I saw her snatch this morning, and it was amazing.

—Pat Glenn, weight lifting commentator

• Ardiles strokes the ball like it's part of his own anatomy.

—Jimmy Magee

• They'll be watching Mike Tyson with a fine-tooth comb from now on.

—Len Boros

• I think he got the stick in the nose. He broke his nose earlier, and it looks as though it's the same nose that he injured before.

—Maurice Couture

• The lead car is absolutely unique, except for the one behind it, which is identical.

—*Murray Walker*

• Sure there have been injuries and deaths in boxing, but none of them serious.

—*Alan Minter*

• If history repeats itself, I should think we can expect the same thing again.

—*Terry Venables*

• The racecourse is as level as a billiard ball.

—*John Francombe*

• When the final horn sounded, Canada's alternate captain, Haley Wickenhauser, threw her gloves in the air along with her elated teammates.

—*Mary Barnes*

• Take note of the way Virginia Wade stands there, her legs spread apart, crouching deeply, with her backside sticking out, waiting to receive serve.

—*Cecil Huntley*

• There goes Juantorena down the back straight, opening his legs and showing his class.

—*David Coleman*

• What will you do when you leave football, Jack? Will you stay in football?

—*Stuart Hall*

- Well, either side could win it, or it could be a draw.

—Ron Atkinson

- Strangely, in slow motion replay, the ball seemed to hang in the air for even longer.

—David Acfield

THE HALL OF FAME OF YOGI BERRAISMS

- It ain't over till it's over.
- Sometimes you can observe a lot by watching.
- No wonder nobody comes here—it's too crowded.
- If people don't want to come out to the ballpark, nobody's gonna stop them.
- A nickel ain't worth a dime anymore.
- Ninety-nine percent of this game is half-mental.

The visiting monster today is Rev. Jack Bains.

Not a Prayer

The appointment of a new pastor happened to coincide with the church's appeal for aid for victims of a hurricane. Unfortunately, on the pastor's first Sunday in the parish, the center page of the church bulletin was accidentally omitted. So members of the congregation read from the bottom of the second page to the top of the last page: "Welcome to the Rev. Andrew Jensen and his family, the worst disaster to hit the area in this century. The full extent of the tragedy is not yet known."

It is sometimes said that if something is perfectly true, then it's exact opposite must also be perfectly true. Bearing this theorem in mind, let us consider Alexander Pope's classic observation "to err is human, to forgive divine."

We turn it inside out, and sure enough: "To err is divine, and to forgive is human." Doubt it? Then wait till you've read the following bloopers, taken from church bulletins, notices, and sermons across our land. See if you don't find yourself forgiving these errors, which, it can be argued, are simply divine.

The especially pious need not fear their responses to these rib-ticklers. It was, after all, Martin Luther who once said, "If I am not allowed to laugh in heaven, I don't want to go there."

• We are especially thankful that when Sister Dora was at death's door, the Lord and her doctors pulled her through.

• Carol and Bob Lehman will be going to Zimbabwe to spread the good words of the Good Book. We congratulate Carol and Bob for assuming their missionary position.

• Attend and you will hear an excellent speaker and heave a healthy lunch.

• In the interest of uniformity and good taste, all worshipers are requested to permit ushers to eat them.

• Reverend Brown announced that after the program they would have a potluck supper. All women giving milk are asked to come early.

• Ladies, remember the HDC Christmas party at our house Friday the 19th, beginning at 7:00 P.M. Potluck supper will be served. Bring your husband and gifts to exchange.

• The church will host an evening of fine dining, superb entertainment, and gracious hostility.

• Reverend Hammond was congratulated on being able to get his parish plastered.

• Church school at 9:45 A.M. We begin a new year with a new curriculum on Sunday. This is a good time to start that child that you promised yourself for so long.

• Man was sent into this world to earn his living by the sweat of his brow. You didn't find Adam walking about the Garden of Eden with his hands in his pockets!

- Everyone is excited about the upcoming wedding of Brad and Melody. They are having a country-style wedding. Everyone is invited to join them as they exchange cows in the church courtyard June 7.
- Sarah Putnam is poorly this spring. Her face is much missed in church, it being always there when she was able to be present.
- The pastor reports 17 weddings, 9 baptisms, and 26 funerals during the year just ended. The year has been a good one, with many causes for rejoicing.
- Sunday breakfast meeting has been planned for the official board of the church, with the Reverend Mr. McCoy undressing the group.
- The Tuesday Night Ladies Club had a lovely time at the church after their potluck supper. For the first time in many months, all members were pregnant.
- We are studying for our Sunday School lesson, "The Ten Virgins." "Each one bring one" is the slogan of our Sunday school.
- Please place your donation in the envelope, along with the deceased person(s) you want remembered.
- This evening at 7:00 P.M. there will be a hymn-sing in the park across from the church. Bring a blanket and come prepared to sin.
- The Advent Retreat will be held in the lover level of St. Mary's Cathedral.

- Sermon outline:
  I. Delineate your fear.
  II. Disown your fear.
  III. Displace your rear.

- When parking on the north side of the church, please remember to park at an angel.
- I am the resurrection and the life. Whosoever believes in me, even though he diets, yet he shall live.
- Glory to God in the highest, and on earth peach to men.
- Hymn: "I am Thin, O Lord."

- Hymn: "What a friend we have in Jesus, all our sins and briefs to bear."
- Hymn: "I Love Thee, My Ford."
- Last hymn in the order of service: "Jesus, Remember Me" (if time permits).
- November 11: An evening of boweling at Lincoln Country Club.
- Please welcome Pastor Don, a caring individual who loves hurting people.
- Next Friday we will be serving hot gods for lunch.
- If you would like to make a donation, fill out a form, enclose a check, and drip in the collection basket.
- Women's Luncheon: Each member bring a sandwich. Polly Phillips will give the medication.
- Congratulations to Tim and Ronda on the birth of their daughter October 12 through 17.
- We are sorry to announce that Mr. Albert Brown has been quite unwell, owing to his recent death, and is taking a short holiday to recover.
- The minister said that the church widows were a disgrace to the parish and that it was time somebody washed them.
- Our youth basketball team is back in action Wednesday at 8:00 P.M. in the recreation hall. Come out and watch us kill Christ the King.
- We are grateful for the help of those who cleaned up the grounds around the church building and the rectum.
- As soon as the weather clears up, the men will have a goof outing.
- Sign-up sheet for anyone wishing to be water-baptized on the table in the foyer.
- Helpers are needed! Please sign up on the information sheep.
- Fifth Sunday is Lent. Thank you, dead friends.
- Diana and Don request your presents at their wedding.
- Bless the Lord, O my soul, and do not forget all His benefits. For the word of God is quick and powerful, piercing even to the dividing asunder of soup and spirit.
- We pray that our people will jumble themselves.

- Pregnancy Information: Any young lady who wants to get pregnant should see Father John at the rectory.
- Volunteers needed: *From a religious institution:* We don't have the man powder to shop and bring this food to our church food pantry.
- Child care provided with reservations.
- Mark your calendars not to attend the church retreat.
- I was hungry and you gave me something to eat; I was thirty, and you gave me drink.
- The visiting monster today is Rev. Jack Bains.
- We are always happy to have you sue our facility.
- We would like to welcome all the brethren and sistern to our church.
- The activity will take place on the church barking lot.
- Sex and Love Addicts Anonymous meets Wednesdays at 7:00 P.M. at St. John's Church. Use rear entrance.
- Next Sunday is the family hayride and bonfire at the Fowlers'. Bring your own hot dogs and guns. Friends are welcome! Everyone come for a fun time.
- Don't forget that elections for head deacon and dead deaconness will be held at next month's business meeting.
- There will not be any Women Worth Watching this week.
- The boars of trustees will meet next Tuesday at 7:00 P.M.
- Jean will be leading a weight-management series Wednesday nights. She's used the program herself and has been growing like crazy!

THE CHURCH BULLETIN HALL OF FAME

- The Ladies' Bible Study will be held Thursday morning at 10:00. All ladies are invited to lunch in the Fellowship Hall after the B.S. is done.
- Missionary Bertha Belch will be speaking at Calvary Memorial Church. Come tonight and hear Bertha Belch all the way from Africa.
- Barbara Chisholm remains in the hospital and needs blood donors for more transfusions. She is also having trouble sleeping and requests tapes of Pastor Jack's sermons.
- Would the congregation please note that the bowl in the back of the church labeled "For the Sick" is for monetary donations only.
- Smile at someone who is hard to love. Say "hell" to someone who doesn't care much about you.
- A bean supper will be held Saturday evening in the church basement. Music will follow.

*The rest of them won't have anything to do with me. They act like that
I got bluebonnet plague.*

Law and Disorder

As a noted British magistrate so accurately observed back in the
1920s, "The criminal court is the most sorrowful place on earth."
But it turns out that many folks facing the music of our justice system manage to rise above the grim occasion and—intentionally or
otherwise—fire off a funny line or two. They bring much-needed
mirth to an otherwise darksome setting.

How else to explain the following exchanges that actually took
place as part of the legal process and were transcribed by court re-
porters, America's keepers of the word? I congratulate them for

keeping a straight face while recording these "transquips" and challenge you to show the same degree of self-restraint as you read these court jests:

THE COURT: I know you, don't I?
DEFENDANT: Uh, yes, Your Honor.
THE COURT: All right, tell me, how do I know you?
DEFENDANT: Judge, do I have to tell you?
THE COURT: Of course, you might be obstructing justice not to tell me.
DEFENDANT: Okay. I was your bookie.

◎

THE COURT: The charge here is theft of frozen chickens. Are you the defendant?
DEFENDANT: No, sir, I'm the guy who stole the chickens.

◎

THE COURT: Well, sir. I have reviewed this case, and I've decided to give your wife $775 each week.
HUSBAND: That's fair, Your Honor. I'll try to send her a few bucks myself.

◎

LAWYER: How do you feel about defense attorneys?
JUROR: I think they should all be drowned at birth.
LAWYER: Well, then, you are obviously biased for the prosecution.
JUROR: That's not true. I think prosecutors should be drowned at birth, too.

◎

THE COURT: Is there any reason you could not serve as a juror in this case?

JUROR: I don't want to be away from my job that long.

THE COURT: Can't they do without you at work?

JUROR: Yes, but I don't want them to know it.

Q. Tell us about the fight.

A. I didn't see no fight.

Q. Well, tell us what you did see.

A. I went to a dance at the Turner house, and as the men swung around and changed partners, they would slap each other, and one fellow hit harder than the other one liked, and so the other one hit back, and somebody pulled a knife and a rifle that had been hidden under a bed, and the air was filled with yelling and smoke and bullets.

LAWYER: Do you think you can be a fair and impartial juror in this trial?

JUROR: Sure.

LAWYER: Do you know the defendant?

JUROR: Yeah.

LAWYER: How well do you know him?

JUROR: Well, not too well. Just to speak to him and stuff.

LAWYER: When was the last time you saw the defendant before this date?

JUROR: Let's see. Oh, yeah. It was the day we stole the money.

JUDGE: Please identify yourself for the record.

DEFENDANT: Col. Ebenezer Jackson.

JUDGE: What does the "Colonel" stand for?

DEFENDANT: Well, it's kinda like the "Honorable" in front of your name—not a damn thing.

DEFENDANT (after being sentenced to 90 days in jail): Can I address the court?

JUDGE: Of course.

DEFENDANT: If I called you a son of a bitch, what would you do?

JUDGE: I'd hold you in contempt and assess an additional five days in jail.

DEFENDANT: What if I thought you were a son of a bitch?

JUDGE: I can't do anything about that. There's no law against thinking.

DEFENDANT: In that case, I think you're a son of a bitch.

◎

Q. Officer, what position was the defendant in while he was being searched?

A. He had two hands on the wall, sir, and two on the ground.

◎

Q. Where do you live?

A. 2442 Oseawotamire Street.

Q. How do you spell that street?

A. S-T-R-E-E-T.

◎

Q. Can you write?

A. Yes, sir, I can write a little.

Q. Have you ever been in a penitentiary?

A. Yes, sir.

Q. What for?

A. Forgery.

◎

Q. Have you ever had any trouble with the law?

A. Not for no reckless driving or speeding or anything like that.

Q. Have you ever been in the penitentiary?

A. I have.

Q. What have you been in the penitentiary for?

A. For murder.

◎

Q. Well, when you say "family," are you limiting yourself to his brother?

A. The rest of them won't have anything to do with me. They act like I got bluebonnet plague.

◎

Q. Who were you living with?

A. My parents.

Q. Did you have any siblings living with you at the time?

A. Just my brothers and sisters.

◎

Q. And, Doctor, as a result of your examination of the plaintiff in this case, was the young lady pregnant?

A. The young lady was pregnant, but not as a result of my examination.

◎

Q. Did you have an appreciable amount of money with you at that time?

A. Whatever money I had I appreciated.

◎

Q. When was the last time you saw him as a chiropractor?

A. I don't know. Every time I see him he's a chiropractor.

◎

Q. Other than traffic court convictions, have you ever pleaded guilty to or been convicted of a felony or misdemeanor?

A. Mr. Who?

Q. Misdemeanor.

A. Who's Mr. Meanor?

THE HALL OF FAME
OF STUPID LAWYER QUESTIONS

- At the time you first saw Dr. McCarty, had you ever seen him prior to that time?
- Did he kill you?
- Doctor, how many autopsies have you performed on dead people?
- You were there until the time you left—is that true?
- In your opinion, how far apart were these vehicles at the time of collision?

Patient is to remain plastered for the next six-to-eight weeks.

Prescriptions for Trouble

While hospitalized, a four-year-old girl asked her mother, "Why are they always playing hide-and-seek here in the hospital?"

"How do they do that?" asked her puzzled mom.

The little girl was unable to clarify what she meant, but soon the explanation was heard over the public address system: "Dr. Blank, ICU; Dr. Blank, ICU."

"See," said the girl, with a vindicated tone.

Well, Dr. Blank, Dr. Who, and Dr. X, I see you—in the transcripts that you dictate.

While I understand how unlikely it is that you, gentle readers, are inclined to regard as funny anything whatsoever associated with the term *medical blooper,* trust me: that's about to change. Because while the things health professionals *do* are certainly serious in nature, sometimes what they say and write *about* what they do would leave Frankenstein in, well, stitches.

It's easiest to suppose that those guilty of such medical muddles ought to have their heads examined. But if their slips of the tongue—but not the tongue depressors—result in nothing more serious than our funny bone (known as the humerus, of course) getting tickled (or even our legs being pulled), there's no need for us to get bent out of shape. For it's by this means that we're afforded a healthy dose of what is, after all, widely recognized as the very best medicine of all.

Jest for the health of it, here's a sampling of malpracticed medical transcriptions. These flashes of premedicated humor will help relieve the tension and dispel the gloom often associated with hospitals and doctors' offices:

- The patient had no recollection of any memory loss.
- The shoulder dislocation was relocated in the emergency room.
- We deferred her pelvic exam until we could get her down to the floor.
- This is a well-developed elderly female. She is oriented to the year, and unsure of where she is. She is unsure of the president, but mentions Hulk Hogan as a possibility.
- While in ER, she was examined, x-rated, and sent home.
- Examination of the patient's foot revealed a hammertoma.
- She had difficulty completing simple calculations. For example, when I asked her what three times three plus one equals, she said, "Ten."
- She stated that she had been constipated for most of her life, until she got a divorce.

- His gait is still unsteady, and, unfortunately, his already painful great toe on the left had an encounter with a dresser, which was unharmed.
- The patient states that diarrhea tends to run in his family.
- No one saw any slurred speech after he awoke.
- Patient is to remain plastered for the next six-to-eight weeks.
- She should continue to wear her tennis elbow.
- She was the driver of a vehicle that was wearing her seat belt.
- His prognosis was poor, having a massive cerebral hemorrhoid.
- A 65-year-old male with proven eosinophilic gastroenteritis was followed for nearly 7 years.
- This lady called saying her neck was increasing in size where we took it off.
- I've authorized two more trips to the chiropractor to help finish him off.
- The patient resides in a nursing home that toppled over, resulting in a broken hip.
- The patient was brought in by two police officers in handcuffs.
- The patient is passing urine adequately on the floor.
- The patient is tearful and crying constantly. She also appears to be depressed.
- I have been following him because of his paranoia.
- I discussed the physiology of Viagra with the patient at length.
- Her mother looked at her ears today and brings them in today to be checked.
- He was given a prescription for Keflex if the ear suddenly comes back.
- The patient had a similar episode in the past when she was exposed to cats with severe wheezing.
- He has no bleeding from the ears or noses.
- The patient had a normal spontaneous vaginal delivery by C-section.
- The patient is a farmer and fell off a concubine.
- He hurt his hip, leg, and growing area.

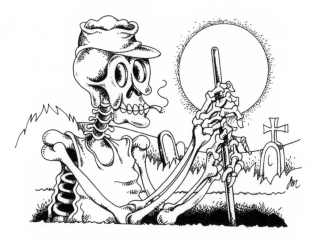

Due to the grave-diggers' strike, all grave digging for the duration will be done by a skeleton crew.

Signs That Should Resign

Most of us are inclined to heed the gazillion signs we see on any given day because we assume that their informative directives are both reliable and intended for our benefit. We trust we'll be displeased with the results of accelerating when we see a STOP sign. We're confident no glistening, bouncing aerobics instructor awaits us at the Rest Area. We understand that "No U-turn" means that it would be entirely irresponsible of us to make a U-turn, especially with traffic hurtling at us from the opposite lane.

Besides the fact that they convey important information, what's also true about the language of signs (and also sign language, come to think of it) is that it's refreshingly concise. No one pulls over to ponder the deeper complexities of "Falling Rocks." "Right Lane Must Turn Right" isn't terribly baffling. "No Parking" is the ultimate, fast-acting option eliminator.

That's what a good sign does: It communicates a simple, helpful message simply. Most of the time, anyway.

About the following real-life signs, I have only one thing to say—"Wrong Way":

• *In the offices of a loan company:* Ask about our plans for owning your home.

• *At a railroad station:* Beware! To touch these wires is instant death. Anyone found doing so will be prosecuted.

• *In a cemetery:* Due to the grave-diggers' strike, all grave digging for the duration will be done by a skeleton crew.

• *On a garage:* Paint your truck for the price of a car.

• *On a golf course:* Any persons (except players) caught collecting golf balls on this course will be prosecuted and have their balls removed.

• *In an optician's office:* Contact lens patients should remember to bring their lenses with them, or we will be unable to see them.

• *On a North Carolina highway:* Permitted Trucks Not Allowed.

• *Above a dryer in a coin laundry:* When the light goes on, please remove all your clothes.

• *At a gym:*

> THE WORLD'S LARGEST WOMEN'S
> FITNESS AND WEIGHT LOSS FRANCHISE

• *In a police canteen in Christchurch, New Zealand:* Will the person who took a slice of cake from the Commissioner's Office return it immediately? It is needed as evidence in a poisoning case.

- *At a medical facility:* Mental Health Prevention Center
- *In a men's room:* Put only toilet paper in toilets. All other matter should go in wastebasket.
- *On a restaurant:* In two weeks this store will become a fruit and vegetable.
- *In a dressing room:* Please return clothing to desk. Don't hang yourself.
- *In a mess hall:* Please give us your feed back.
- *In a bookstore:* Sex/Self-Help
- *On a ski slope:* Out-of-control skiers yield right-of-way.
- *On a dry cleaner's:* Drop your pants and skirts here, and you will receive prompt attention.
- *In another dry-cleaning store:* Anyone leaving their garments here for more than 30 days will be disposed of.
- *On a bookstore:* Rare, out-of-print, and nonexistent books
- *Posted near a film drop:* Allow an extra day for overnight service.
- *In a pizzeria:* Proceeds from sales of carved ducks go to handicap children.
- *In a restaurant:* Open seven days a week and weekends.
- *In an office:* After the tea break staff should empty the teapot and stand upside down on the draining board.
- *On a highway:*

```
POLISH
FOOT-LONG
CHEESEBURGERS
```

- *In a supermarket:* Self-checkout available for your convenience. Ask for assistance.
- *At another supermarket:* Only service dogs allowed in building.

One of my favorite categories of sign bloopers is the multiple listing, in which words collide:

- *On a store:*

> LIQUOR STORE
> EATS
> SPORTING GOODS

- *In another store:*

> SENIOR CITIZENS
> BUY ONE, GET ONE FREE!

- *On the door of a fast-food restaurant:*

> NO
> PETS
> SHIRTS
> SHOES
> REQUIRED

- *On a movie theater marquee:*

> ERIN BROCKOVICH
> SCREWED
> MY DOG SKIP

- *On a gas station:*

```
NOW HIRING
CHICKEN DINNERS
```

When a woman announced her impending marriage at the age of 40, the proprietor of a chain of Chinese restaurants where she had worked for 20 years asked that he be allowed to give the wedding reception.

After the marriage ceremony, the guests approached the restaurant, where the happy owner greeted them outside the front door. With great dignity he opened the door to reveal a banner hanging inside bearing the enthusiastic greeting: MAY YOU HAVE AN ENJOYABLE CHANGE OF LIFE.

THE HALL OF FAME OF SIGN LANGUAGE

- Shoes are required to eat inside.
- Help keep the birds healthy. Don't feed them restaurant food.
- We don't tear your clothing with machinery. We do it carefully by hand.
- Don't take a chance on ruining your vacation. Come to us and be sure.
- This door is alarmed 24 hours a day.

```
GIANT BLUEBERRIES
SQUASH
NATIVE CORN
```

Eating rocks may lead to broken teeth.

Warning:
Loony Labels

Manufacturers of consumer products have to be liberal with the warning labels nowadays, lest they get sued. In the 21st century, people actually file lawsuits against McDonald's and other fast-food chains claiming that what they ate in those establishments made them fat in the waist, weak in the heart, and clogged in the arteries. For years these unsuspecting customers have been wandering into these restaurants thinking that they served health food and have been receiving hamburgers and french fries instead of celery stalks and carrot sticks.

Frivolous lawsuits are a boon for devious lawyers and warning-label writers. To protect the public from injury—and themselves from lawsuits—many manufacturers include warning labels on their products. Some of these labels alert consumers to unimaginable dangers:

- *On a package of five-inch fishing lures:* Harmful if swallowed.
- *On a 12-inch-high storage rack for compact discs:* Do not use as a ladder.
- *On a snow sled:* Sled may develop high speed under certain snow conditions.
- *On a package of frozen food:* Defrost your frozen dinner before eating.
- *On a lawn mower:* When motor is running, the blade is turning.
- *On a bottle of spray paint:* Do not spray in your face.
- *On a container of salt:* Warning: High in sodium.
- *On a Eureka vacuum cleaner:* Caution: Assemble the cleaner before using.
- *On a package containing a rubber ball:* Choking hazard: This toy is a small ball.
- *On a fireplace log:* Caution—risk of fire.
- *On a public toilet:* Recycled flush water unsafe for drinking.
- *On a package of dishwasher liquid:* Do not allow children to play in the dishwater.
- *On a baby stroller:* Remove child before folding.
- *On a neck wrap designed to be heated in a microwave:* Do not microwave while on body.
- *On a container of pepper spray:* May irritate eyes.
- *On a laser printer cartridge:* Do not eat toner.
- *On a package of rock garden materials:* Eating rocks may lead to broken teeth.

- *On a carpenter's electric router:* This product not intended for use as a dental drill.
- *On a bottle of dog shampoo:* Cruelty-free. Not tested on animals.
- *On a jet ski:* Warning! Riders of personal watercraft may suffer injury due to the forceful injection of water into body cavities either by falling into the water or while mounting the craft.
- *On a blanket:* Not to be used as protection from a tornado.
- *On a hair dryer:* Do not use in shower.
- *On a curling iron:* This product can burn eyes.
- *On a coffee cup:* Caution: Hot beverages are hot!
- *On a toilet bowl cleaning brush:* Do not use orally.
- *On a snowblower:* Do not use blower on roof.
- *In the manual for a microwave oven:* Do not use for drying pets.
- *On a package of Silly Putty:* Do not use as earplugs.
- *On a bottle of Tylenol arthritis pain medication:* Do not use for more than ten days unless directed by a doctor eight years of age.
- *On the packaging of a sharpening stone:* Warning: Knives are sharp!
- *On a pack of Breath Savers:* Not for weight control.
- *On a tube of deodorant:* Do not use intimately.
- *On a box of rat poison:* Has been found to cause cancer in laboratory mice.
- *On a box of Midol PMS relief tablets:* Warning: Do not use if you have prostate problems.
- *In the instructions for an electric thermometer:* Do not use orally after using rectally.
- *On the bottom of a wind-up kitchen timer:* Do not place on or near heat-producing appliances.
- *On a box of bottle rockets:* Do not put in mouth.
- *On the back of a cardboard windshield, for keeping the car from getting too hot when parked:* Please remove before driving.
- *On the wrapper of a Fruit Roll-Up snack:* Remove plastic before eating.

- *On a TV remote control:* Not dishwasher safe.
- *On the packaging for a wristwatch:* Warning! This is not underwear! Do not attempt to put in pants.
- *In the manual for a massage chair:* Never force any body part into the backrest area of the massage chair while the rollers are moving.
- *On a rest room dryer:* Do not activate with wet hands.
- *On a battery:* Do not recharge, put in backwards, or use.
- *On a bottle of bathtub cleaner:* For best results, start with a clean tub before use.
- *On a plastic orange juice container:* 100 percent pure all-natural fresh-squeezed orange juice from concentrate.
- *On the back of a can of deicing windshield fluid:* Cannot be made nonpoisonous.
- *On a Table Top charcoal grill:* Do not place on top of any table.
- *On a window fan:* Do not place fan in window.
- *On a computer software package:* Optional modem required.
- *On an Aim-n-Flame fireplace lighter:* Do not use near fire, flame, or sparks.
- *On a Frisbee:* Warning: May contain small parts.
- *On the bottom of a Coke bottle:* Do not open here.
- *On a bottle of drain cleaner:* If you do not understand, or cannot read, all directions, cautions, and warnings, do not use this product.

This is why this genre of bloopers inspires such brilliant satire:

> *I wish to complain. The instructions on your deodorant were very misleading. I followed your instructions on a stick of deodorant to the letter: "Take Off Top, Push Up Bottom," and was left seminaked in some not inconsiderable pain. And it didn't help my perspiring.*
>
> *It's time that the writers of these instructions take responsibility for the resulting actions. The claim on the front, "Sure Won't Let You Down," was correct. I was unable to sit down all morning.*

THE HALL OF FAME
OF WARNING LABELS

- *On a Sears hair dryer:* Do not use while sleeping.
- *On a Zippo lighter:* Do not ignite in face.
- *On a Pop-Tart box:* Warning—filling may be hot when heated.
- *On packaging for a Rowenta iron:* Do not iron clothes on body.
- *On a packet of Nytol sleeping aids:* Warning—may cause drowsiness.
- *On a box of rest room towel rollers:* Warning! Improper use may cause injury or death!

The Power
of the Press

Aging Conference Speakers Address the Old Problems

Double-Trouble Headlines

You're walking along, your eyes sweep across the newspaper in a stand, and boom!—you're informed. You've learned all you really need to know about that day's Big Stories from the paper's headlines!

Those headlines didn't make you an expert on their stories. The 2.2 seconds you spent gulping down those headlines aren't going to get you invited to be a guest panelist on *Meet the Press*. But now you're ready for office chat around the water cooler or in the lunch line.

Why? Because some dedicated, deadline-crazed journalist somewhere diligently banged his head upon his desk blotter until a decent headline fell out. And in clear, catchy, concise, controlled, communicative capitals, that headline captured the crucial content of that account.

Because that's what headlines are for. That's what they *do*.

Except, of course, for those rare occasions when they make you feel as if *you've* been banging your head on something—and are now seeing double.

It's the awful lot of an awful lot of English words to have more than one meaning. Sometimes that's a good thing. And sometimes, as in the headlines below, it's a downright delightful thing—as long as you're not the responsible editor-in-grief. Witness how the double meaning of a word or two can inadvertently change a serious journalist into a silly play-write:

ENERGY EXECUTIVES URGE SOME
GAS-ELIMINATION LIMITS ON BUSH

◎

FOUR TOP DOGS INDUCTED INTO
MEAT INDUSTRY HALL OF FAME

◎

BANK DRIVE-IN WINDOW BLOCKED BY BOARD

◎

OFFICIALS SUSPENDED OVER HOTEL FIRE

◎

LAWMAKERS BACK TRAIN THROUGH IOWA

◎

EGG PLANT MUST PAY DAMAGES FOR FLY PROBLEM

◎

POLICE GRILL SUICIDAL MAN
AFTER SCHOOLBOY SET ON FIRE

◎

ASIAN POPULATION JUMPS ACROSS COUNTRY

◎

JAPANESE SCIENTISTS GROW FROG EYES AND EARS

◎

CITIZENS GET SHOT AT NEW CONSERVATORY

◎

SLAIN WOMAN TIED TO KANSAS MAN AT TRIAL

◎

JAPANESE STILL EYEING HAWAII

◎

MILLIONS HELD BY FORMER ENRON EXEC, KIN FROZEN

◎

LACK OF BRAINS HINDERS RESEARCH

◎

BOAT CAPTAIN FISHES FOR FAMILY

◎

COMPANIES GRAPPLE WITH WORKPLACE VIOLENCE

◎

DENVER CHAPTER WILL HAVE SENATOR FOR BREAKFAST

QUARTER OF A MILLION CHINESE LIVE ON WATER

REPORTS ON BIN LADEN DRYING UP

ESTIRIN TO LEAVE CISCO SYSTEMS TO LAUNCH
HER FOURTH START-UP WITH HER HUSBAND

NEW VACCINE TO CONTAIN RABIES

SURVIVOR OF SIAMESE TWINS JOINS PARENTS

NEW STUDY OF OBESITY LOOKS FOR LARGER TEST GROUP

DRUG TRAFFIC REACHES NEW HIGH

MUNICIPAL SEATS UP FOR GRABS

CROUPIERS ON STRIKE—MANAGEMENT: "NO BIG DEAL"

MANY SEEK RELIEF FROM VALLEY SOCIAL AGENCIES

COACH DROPS BALL ON HEAD INJURIES

DODGE SAYS PROBE PUTS HIM IN AWKWARD POSITION

COURT RULES LAW ON NUDE REPRODUCTION TOO BROAD

MORE TEENS GET SHOT AT ADVANCED CLASSES

AGING CONFERENCE SPEAKERS
ADDRESS THE OLD PROBLEMS

ANTHRAX REPORTS SWELL

CITIZENS COMPLAIN ABOUT LOUD NOISE AT CITY MEETING

CLEANERS DROP SUIT

1.6 MILLION CHEROKEES ARE RECALLED

DRUG FIRM SELLS 2 LINES TO RIVALS

RESERVES, NATIONAL GUARD:
WHO CAN KEEP THEM STRAIGHT?

CHICAGO CHECKING ON ELDERLY IN HEAT

◎

BRITISH FOOT-IN-MOUTH REMEDY: MASSIVE SLAUGHTER

◎

THE IMPORTANCE OF BONDAGE
BETWEEN VOTER AND GOVERNMENT

◎

ASSAILANT DIES AFTER KNIFE TURNED ON HIM

◎

JUDGE HONORED FOR JUVENILE WORK

◎

CUBANS MARCH OVER 6-YEAR-OLD

◎

NEED TO BREED SPURS BIRD CALL FROM QUEEN

◎

GAS LEVELS HIGH IN BEANTOWN

◎

FETUS DETERMINED TO BE PART OF MOTHER'S BODY

◎

MOVE TO BAN BOOKS GROWING IN TEXAS

Sometimes a hapless headline causes readers to throw up their hands and ask, "Huh?" because the message lacks anything in the way of apparent logic. For example, a story once appeared about the death of Dr. J. Julian Chisolm, Jr., whose research into lead poisoning in children caused by peeling paint is credited with saving thousands if not millions of lives. The head-scratching headline blared: POISONING RESEARCHER CREDITED WITH SAVING LIVES.

Here are some more of my favorite blinkers, those "How's that again?" headlines:

BUSH ROARS INTO TOWN; FORD HAS STROKE

◎

NO CAUSE OF DEATH DETERMINED FOR BEHEADED VICTIM

◎

NEW ORLEANS DODGES STORM'S PATH

◎

TULANE CENTER MONKEYS ESCAPE;
HALF ARE CAPTURED IN TIME FOR DINNER

◎

WALL STREET: REST OF THE YEAR
MAY NOT FOLLOW JANUARY

◎

ONE-LEGGED RAPIST STILL ON RUN

◎

BOARD SEATS RUN UNOPPOSED

◎

DUNCAN TO MISS 4 GAMES AFTER HIS FATHER DIES

◎

LEE PRIEST ON LEAVE FOR SEX WITH WORKER

◎

CASTRO MARKS 75 YEARS IN VENEZUELA JUNGLE

◎

THE BAD DREAM OF TOO FEW TEACHERS IS COMING TRUE

◎

PHILADELPHIA POLICE TO TOW 1,000 CARS FOR 40 DAYS

◎

NRC: FUEL RODS MISTAKENLY STORED IN SAFE PLACE

◎

NO PUNISHMENT TOO HARSH FOR MOOSE LAKE RESIDENTS

◎

DEATH PENALTY MEASURE PROVIDES FOR
ELECTROCUTION FOR ALL PERSONS OVER 17

◎

SENATOR WANTS TOUGHER DEATH PENALTY

◎

WOMAN QUIZZED AFTER DEATH

◎

INSANITY PLEA BY MAN WHO'S HIS OWN LAWYER

◎

BONUS PERMITS ENABLE 809 HUNTERS TO KILL 2 DEER

◎

SEEK HELP, CONFIDE IN SPOUSE
BEFORE EMBARKING ON AFFAIR

MICROSOFT ACCUSES FEDERAL JUDGE OF BEING IMPARTIAL

COPS QUIZ VICTIM IN FATAL SHOOTING

RITALIN MAY HELP PREVENT DRUG USE

SWIMSUIT JUDGING CALLED GOOD FOR FITNESS

DEAD YOUTH IN SERIOUS MEDICAL CONDITION

25 YEARS IN PRISON FOR MAN
WHO KILLED, THEN BLINDED WITNESS

It is but a short leap to those blinding glimpses into the obvious that cause readers to respond, while scratching their head and rolling their eyes, "Quite so. What's the big deal?":

PARENTS' CRUCIAL ROLE IN FAMILY STRESSED

FEDERAL AGENTS RAID GUN SHOP, FIND WEAPONS

LIVING DONORS OUTPACE DEAD DONORS

PROSTATE CANCER MORE COMMON IN MEN

OLDER BLACKS HAVE EDGE IN LONGEVITY

PHYSICAL ACTIVITY ESSENTIAL TO PREVENT INACTIVITY

LARGER KANGAROOS LEAP FARTHER, RESEARCHERS FIND

MUSLIM CENTER HAS ISLAMIC TIES

THE HALL OF FAME OF TWO-HEADED HEADLINES

MAN STRUCK BY LIGHTNING
FACES BATTERY CHARGE

KIDS MAKE NUTRITIOUS SNACKS

QUEEN MARY HAVING BOTTOM SCRAPED

HIGH COURT TO HEAR MARIJUANA CASE

LEGISLATORS TAX BRAINS TO CUT DEFICIT

4-H GIRLS WIN PRIZES FOR FAT CALVES

War Worries Dog Senators

Banner Grammar Stammers

Most kids hate learning grammar. "Subjects, nouns and verbs, subjects and direct objects, commas and apostrophes—who cares!" goes up the cry. "As long as a person can tell what's being said, what difference does it make?"

If you're a teacher (professionally or spiritually), I'd like to suggest that the next time you're facing such a protest, you throw out to your class or listeners TEACHERS STRIKE IDLE KIDS. Then explain, "This headline was actually published in a newspaper. As we can see, there is something about it that is grotesquely wrong. Now are we all absolutely *certain* that grammar doesn't matter one single bit?"

To be further convincing, you could also write, STOLEN PAINTING FOUND BY TREE or ENRAGED COW INJURES FARMER WITH AXE. Each, alas, is a bona fide banner boner. And so are the following grammar gaffes, each of which comes up one pica short of a clear statement:

PARENT DEMAND FOR TRAINING MUSHROOMS

❀

SMOKING MORE HAZARDOUS THAN THOUGHT

❀

BUSH: WE KNOW IRAQ HAS BANNED WEAPONS

❀

TWO AFGHAN WOMEN POLL WORKERS KILLED IN BLAST

❀

JUDGE FACING SEX CHARGES AHEAD IN EARLY RETURNS

❀

WARMEST WEEKEND AHEAD IN SIX MONTHS

❀

DISTRICT ATTORNEY DECLINES TO TRY SHOOTING SUSPECT

❀

WAR WORRIES DOG SENATORS

❀

MAN SOLD WHILE BABY NULLIFIES ADOPTION

❀

COP ACCUSED OF FORCING WOMEN TO STRIP SUSPENDED

❧

EDITOR'S WIFE RENTED TO TWO SUSPECTS, FBI SAYS

❧

MAN WHO ROBBED BANK DISGUISED AS
WOMAN FACES 3-6 YEARS

❧

GAME CANCELED AFTER KILE'S DEATH RESCHEDULED

❧

POLICE ARREST TWO JUVENILES AFTER BATTING
ELDERLY WOMAN AND HER NEIGHBOR ON HEADS

❧

MAN HITS DOG ON MOTORCYCLE

❧

FRANÇOIS PLEADS GUILTY TO KILLING
8 WOMEN TO AVOID DEATH PENALTY

❧

STUDY OFERS ANOTHER REASON
TO GET PAP TESTS: RESEARCHERS

❧

POLICE LOOK FOR WITNESS TO RAPE

❧

COUNTY WORKERS GET SUSPICIOUS MAIL TRAINING

❧

COMMUNITY MEETS TO DISCUSS
VIOLENCE AT TOWN HALL MEETING

S.F. POLICE SHOOT MAN WITH KNIFE

PRINCIPAL TRANSFERS UPSET PARENTS

BODY FOUND IN VAN DONATED TO SALVATION ARMY

PANDA LECTURES THIS WEEK AT NATIONAL ZOO

PRODUCE THROWN AT WORKERS WITH CHAIN SAWS

MAN CHARGED WITH MOLESTING
TWIN BROTHER FOUND DEAD IN STORAGE

ACCIDENT ON FREEWAY INVOLVES
4 CARS, HOSPITALIZES ONE

TWO DISCOVER 5-YEAR-OLD ON WAY TO WORK

DOGS HELP TERRORIST ATTACK VICTIMS

FISH MAY FIGHT DEPRESSION WHILE PREGNANT

JURY FAVORS SHOOTING VICTIMS

⊚

DEER KILL OPPONENTS GAINING GROUND
IN LAWSUIT AGAINST GUNMAKERS

⊚

EAST ST. LOUIS POLICE STOP FLEEING GANGSTERS

⊚

KILLER SENTENCED TO DIE
FOR SECOND TIME IN 10 YEARS

⊚

GUN DEALER WANTS GUN SOLD TO McVEIGH

⊚

BLAME FLIES AFTER COLLAPSE OF ARENA BUILDING

⊚

SOVIET VIRGIN LANDS SHORT OF GOAL AGAIN

⊚

MANY BUSINESSES SAY ENGLISH
MUST BE SPOKEN ON BY WORKERS

Closely related to the above category is the presence of the typo or spello gremlins who chitter through many a headline howler:

BUSH EXORCISED, SOURCES SAY

⊚

WANT TO SPELL LIKE A CHAMP?
READ WENSTER'S DICTIONARY

⊚

U.N. PEACEKEEPERS LAND
IN LIBERIA TO REIGN IN VIOLENCE

※

FOUTH-GRADE READING IS MOST DIFFICULT OF TESTS

※

"BARBARA OF SEVILLE" OPENS VALLEY OPERA SEASON

※

SCIENTISTS SPOT PLANT OUTSIDE SOLAR SYSTEM

※

FAMILY FEARS RABIES FROM RAPID KITTEN

※

TWO MEN ARRESTED FOR HEROINE TRAFFICKING

※

KIDS MOST LIKE TO HAVE SELF-INFLICTED WOUNDS

※

GO GET 'EM, EVEN DURING RAMADA

※

BRAIN DRAIN SMALL, BUT SIGNNIFICANT, STUDY SAYS

※

ENVOY CALLS FOR PEACH BEFORE TALKS

※

BRIDE STANDS 46-TON TEST FRIDAY

※

CARDINAL O'CONNOR TO DELIVER HOMINY

A story appeared about a Harvard president who disagreed with planned construction in Harvard Square. Somebody's Freudian slip was showing because the headline atop the article read: COLLEGE PRESIDENT FIGHTS ERECTION IN HARVARD SQUARE. Some headline howlers are simply too lewd, lascivious, and licentious to have been published purposely in family newspapers:

MARRIED PRIESTS IN CATHOLIC CHURCH
A LONG TIME COMING

◎

CLINTON STIFF ON WITHDRAWAL

◎

SMOKING ORGAN CAUSES STIR IN NURSING HOME

◎

CHEERLEADERS COLLAPSE IN HEAT

◎

ANIMAL MOVEMENTS BANNED

◎

FORMER PRESIDENT ENTERS DINAH SHORE

◎

STUDENT EXCITED DAD GOT HEAD JOB

◎

FARMER'S NONSTOP COCK DISTURBS NEIGHBORS

◎

ORGAN FESTIVAL ENDS IN SMASHING CLIMAX

THE HALL OF FAME
OF GRAMMAR STAMMERS

MARRIAGE LICENSES PERMITS MOUNTING

◎

WHY YOU WANT SEX CHANGES WITH AGE

◎

ATTORNEYS GO ALONG
WITH STRIKING WORKERS

◎

PROGRESS SLOW IN BEATING DEATH

◎

TWO CARS COLLIDE,
ONE SENT TO HOSPITAL

◎

RUSSIAN FORCES BEAR DOWN

*Rolls-Royce . . . recalling all . . . cars . . . because of faulty nuts
behind the steering wheels.*

The Daily Bu(n)gle

You're in the pressroom. You're pressed for time. You're wearing clothes you haven't pressed since you quit dating people you tried to impress. The scene can be depressing. You hope to repress its memory.

It's a pressure cooker in there. Phones are roundly ringing. Facts are being faxed. Keyboards are clacking like cacophonous castanets constantly clapped by a cadre of caffeinated cats.

And *words* are driving you crazy. They're all you're thinking about. And to right now write right you need them all. Big, small, medium, rare, well-done, poorly done, impeccably paired, pointedly profound, passionately precise, parenthetically purposeful *words* are what you're praying to produce.

You know the story. You've *got* the story. All you have to do is write it down.

In vain you strain your brain. It's inhumane. What a pain.

Fingers flying, with barely a pause, you bear down on the story like the grizzled veteran you are. No flimflammer, you start to hammer your grammar, tack down your syntax, idiot-proof your idioms, banish your banalities, and hone your tone. Away, gray cliché!

Finally, you have it: irrefutable proof that you, of all people, deserve your room in the Fourth Estate. And so, in truth, do all your fellow mansion-mates—though, as we'll see in the published howlers below, some will have to serve time in the doghouse:

• *Anchorage:* The state board of fisheries is considering whether to impose seasonal catch limits on tourists.

• At Wednesday's luncheon meeting of the Rotary Club, to be held at Chello's Restaurant on the Post Road, Jacob Emery will speak about his experiences in the Arctic. Because of snow and cold weather last Wednesday, Emery was unable to be at the meeting.

• Queen Elizabeth arrived in Paris to begin a visit that inspired the warmest welcome the French have given a royal figure since they guillotined their own Queen Marie Antoinette.

• Rita Hayworth said yesterday that she was flat busted and felt sorry for her husband, Dick Haymes, who has worries of his own.

• Owing to the lack of space and the rush of editing this issue, several births and deaths will be postponed until next week.

• Doris, Agnes, and Vivian Smith are spending several days at the home of their mother. This is the first time in many years that the community has had the pleasure of seeing the Smith girls in the altogether at one time.

• The Colgate-Palmolive Company announced that it will contribute ten cents to the Olympic Fund for the first one million box tops or wrappers collected from specified soaps, detergents, and toiletries between now and July 15.

- In the head-on collision of the two passenger cars, five people were killed in the crash, two seriously.
- Nine presidential candidates exposed themselves in Washington, D.C., before Democratic governors.
- White, 50, admitted that on March 27, 2002, he drove 138 miles to the Wal-Mart where his son-in-law, Aaron Ruboyianes, worked and shot him three times in the electronics department.
- The ladies of the county medical society auxiliary plan to publish a cookbook. Part of the money will go to the Samaritan Hospital to purchase a stomach pump.
- After the sun goes down here, there are practically no recreational facilities for those who are not married.
- Wednesday afternoon, when Ruby Chesterfield stopped by to deliver supplies for the church kitchen, she encountered a young man in the process of robbing the food cabinets. After an extended chase all over the church, she finally caught him by the organ.
- Rolls-Royce announced today that it is recalling all Rolls-Royce cars made after 1966 because of faulty nuts behind the steering wheels.
- One of the central tenets of modern medicine is that the earlier your doctor can catch a disease, the better.
- *SATURDAY'S ANSWER:*
  Did you experience any Y2K technical problems?
  Due to technical difficulties, the results of Saturday's question were not available.
- An outbreak of scabies at the Ann Lee nursing home was contained this week after the facility and its residents were sterilized, officials said Wednesday.
- Both volunteered in 1944 to be kamikaze pilots. They learned to fly, but the war ended before they could make an impact.
- The Pratt School PTA is busily organizing the annual Pratt Fall Festival.
- Lt. Jimmie E. Gibson, wife, and baby left Sunday for Hawaii, where they will be stationed for three years. Friends here hope that they will like their trip and stay in the islands.

• The local medical association made a presentation to the minister complaining of laboratory delays, especially the ten-month wait for a pregnancy test.

• Britain faces an explosion of alcoholism, with the prospect of a million addicts. And most of these will be men and women, says a shock report out yesterday.

• It costs just $25 each year to register your desexed dog in Brisbane and only $10 a year for pensioners.

• Six men, their faces covered with red bandannas, got out of the Cherokee carrying a knife, baseball bat, billy club, and rolling pin, said Davis, 20. "I knew when I saw the rolling pin that something bad was going to go down," Davis said.

• Most power outages have been restored.

• The Salt Lake Track Club's All-Women's 10,000-meter race is scheduled for Saturday at 8:00 A.M. at Sugarhouse Park. The entry fee is four dollars with shirt or one dollar without.

• She was arrested after she was discovered running through the streets of town in the nude. Police held her several days for observation.

• A resolution to install two new fire hydrants was approved by the council. The resolution followed a report by the police department that the dog population during the past year has increased by 26.

• Overcome by gas while taking a bath, she owes her life to the watchfulness of a janitor.

• President Kennedy and the First Lady are expecting their third child, it was learned from a source believed to be responsible.

• Twice a bridegroom and finally a bride was Cheryl Watson.

• She held a special place in her heart for her twin sister, who is two years younger than she.

• The airplane suffered mechanical problems and landed in Switzerland, where the crew was interred for the remainder of the war.

• Joseph Pettit, head of an artificial insemination farm center, had his car wrecked by an angry bull.

• Police believed the well-armed survivalist killed himself before setting his apartment on fire.

- As the forecaster is off the island, there will be no weather this weekend.

- The sewer expansion project is nearing completion, but city officials are holding their breath until it is officially finished.

- Faite Mack, Jr., 56, a professor in the graduate education program at Grand Valley State University, said he has been frustrated by the voters' take on Bush's debate performances. "I'm mystified at how dumb Americans are in thinking Bush won those debates," said the Grand Rapids resident, who declined to give his age.

- Eleven out of the 15 dismissed clerical officers at the Federal Agricultural Research and Training Station (FARTS), Umudike Imuahia, Nigeria, have been reengaged.

- Today there are drug courts in every state. An estimated 300,000 offenders have completed programs. In addition to its adult drug court, Maine has a three-year-old juvenile drug court.

- Families with 12 million children will not qualify in the tax credit this year.

- Simultaneously with Bayes, Belle Cramer is showing some landscapes and still lives.

- The court, presented with no solid evidence to the contrary accepted his testimony that the Great Dane had urinated, not defecated.

- Sir—I write to record my protest at the increasing tendency for sections of an article to be scattered throughout the magazine. It is extremely *(Please turn to page 48.)*

- *From an obituary on British singer Yanna:* In 1960 she played Alice Fitzwarren in "Turn Again Whittington" at the London Palladium, opposite Norman Wisdom's Dick.

- *From an article headlined 2 DIE IN APPARENT MURDER-SUICIDE:* The bodies were found by each other in a house on Shamrock Avenue, said Johnny Shelton of the Surry County Emergency Medical Services, and each had been shot in the chest. Neighbors told investigators that Hawks and Mrs. Jones had been dating since Mrs. Jones's divorce a year ago, but that, following an argument earlier this week, she had told him to pack his thing and leave.

The *Charleston Gazette* once ran a story about political satirist Mark Russell, who finds high-voltage humor in current events, especially the absurdities in Washington, D.C. Included in the report was this paragraph: "Accompanying himself at his star-draped grand piano, the humorist began poking fun at politicians many years ago as the resident comedian at Washington's Shoreham Hotel on Capitol Hill. Today the bow-tied and bespeckled Russell spends most of his time on the road as a stand-up comedian."

The bespectacled, not "bespeckled," Mark Russell probably got a huge laugh when he spotted that one.

THE GALLEY OOPS! HALL OF FAME

- The father was employed at the Seabrook nuclear power plant and commuted for some months. Then the family moved to Seabrook, where they are happily living.
- Columbia, Tennessee, which calls itself the largest outdoor mule market, held a mule parade yesterday headed by the governor.
- The summary of information contains totals of the number of students broken down by sex, age, and marital status.
- An animal rights group that hopes to change America's meat-eating ways scheduled a meeting here today at the Black Angus steakhouse.
- A federal grand jury has accused three women identified by the IRS as topless dancers of concealing their assets.

Unfortunately, the illustrations of edible and poisonous types of mushrooms were reversed on page 14 of our Sunday edition.

Co-wreck-tions

A news story misquoted former First Lady Barbara Bush. The report claimed that Mrs. Bush had joked in a speech that she went through three breast sizes in her lifetime. Barbara Bush had said "dress sizes," and the newspaper ran a correction the following day. Still, it received a letter from Mrs. Bush and printed it in its Sunday editorial page:

> "I've just become abreast of your recent article. I am indeed a bosom buddy of two presidents, so I shared some of the things I have learned in 76 years of life. That includes 57 years of married life, six children, 14 grandchildren, five wars, three DRESS

sizes, two governors, two parachute jumps, and now two presidents.
"Your article has left this generally outspoken mother speechless
but has given my children much to laugh about."

At the end of a typed letter was a handwritten note: "I just wanted to get this off my chest!"

No one likes making mistakes—especially newspaper people, since their bloopers end up right out there, in black and white, for the whole world to see. But although our dedicated news writers, editors, and publishers loathe printing mistakes, their ethics (and their lawyers—but let's not quibble) demand that they quickly, directly, and publicly acknowledge and repair those inaccuracies.

Sometimes the correction process itself does seem to wobble out of control, and the corrections are more clarity-challenged than the original versions. It's like the man who goes to the doctor because of a pain in his back—only to have the doctor rap him on the head with his knuckles. "Ouch!" cries the man. "That really hurt!"

"Yes," says the doctor. "But notice how the pain in your neck is gone!"

The following are all published, bungled attempts to right an original wrong. Ouch:

• Unfortunately, the illustrations of edible and poisonous types of mushrooms were reversed on page 14 of our Sunday edition.

• Last issue we said that "the proceeds of the casserole supper will go to disable veterans." As several people pointed out, that was a mistake. It should have read, "the proceeds of the casserole supper will go to help disable veterans."

• Due to a transcription error in the *Rolling Stone* interview, we mistakenly quoted Bill Clinton using the word *dumbass* when he actually said, "Don't ask," in reference to the "don't ask, don't tell" policy. *Rolling Stone* apologizes to Mr. Clinton for the error.

• A story headlined "Syria Seeks Our Help to Woo U.S." in Saturday's *Weekend Australian* misquoted National Party senator Sandy Macdonald. The quotation stated, "Syria is a country that has been a bastard state for nearly 40 years" but should have read, "Syria is a country that has been a Baathist state for nearly 40 years." The *Australian* regrets any embarrassment caused by the error.

• The name of Grace Shrader, a seventh-grade winner in the *Times* spelling bee, was misspelled in the March 2 Porter County edition. The *Times* regrets the error.

• The picture in Wednesday's issue was inadvertently identified as a taxi bandit. The gentleman is actually the prime minister of Greece.

• Alan Frank Keiser's name was misspelled in Thursday's listing of marriage licenses. He will marry Liduya Demyanovna Savchenko.

• An item in the March 6 *Police News* incorrectly identified the suspect in a dispute incident as the wife of the 43-year-old victim's ex-husband. The suspect is actually the ex-wife of the victim's husband.

• A photo caption in Wednesday's front section identified Rudy Langford of Hampton as chairman of the "Collusion for Justice." There is no such organization. Langford is chairman of the Coalition for Justice.

• An article about the Alano Club incorrectly quoted executive board member Harvey McInness as saying, "We're not AA, we're not Narcotics Anonymous. We're a social outlet where people can come, have coffee, shoot people, visit friends, or maybe go to a coffeehouse." Mr. McInness actually said, ". . . where people can come, have coffee, shoot pool. . . ."

• There was a mistake in an item sent in two weeks ago that stated that Ed Burnham entertained a party at crap shooting. It should have been trap shooting.

• Our *Barnstead Story* series has unfortunately appeared out of sequence. Episode 172, published last week, is followed by episode 174 this week. Part 15 will appear next week and thereafter part 17 and the rest.

• The *Ottawa Citizen and Southam News* wishes to apologize for our apology to Mark Steyn. In correcting the incorrect statements about Mr. Steyn, published October 15, we incorrectly published the incorrect correction. We accept and regret that our original regret was unacceptable, and we apologize to Mr. Steyn for any distress caused by our previous apology.

• The "Greek Special" is a huge 18-inch pizza and not a huge 18-inch penis, as described in an ad in yesterday's *Daily Californian*.

Blondie's Pizza would like to apologize for any confusion Friday's ad may have caused.

• The absence of corrections yesterday was due to a technical hitch rather than any sudden onset of accuracy.

Perhaps the two most bizarre corrections ever published are these from *Harvard Magazine* and the *Canberra Times*, in Australia:

• We have learned that the obituary for Erik Humphrey Gordon, 95, which appeared in the July–August issue, was based on false information by the subject himself in an effort to get off Harvard's mailing list. Mr. Gordon is alive and well and living in New York City.

• For some considerable time, the *Times* has been publishing wrong tide times for Narooma. The error was discovered when the editor, relying on the *Times* figures, was swept out to sea. But he managed to return to shore and ordered this correction.

THE HOUSE OF CORRECTIONS HALL OF FAME

• It was incorrectly reported last Friday that today is T-shirt Appreciation Day. In fact, it is actually Teacher Appreciation Day.

• Our article about Jewish burial customs contained an error: mourners' clothing is rent—that is, torn—not rented.

• In one edition of today's food section, an inaccurate number of jalapeño peppers was given for Jeanette Crowley's southwestern chicken salad recipe. The recipe should call for 2, not 21, jalapeño peppers.

• Erroneous information was inadvertently inserted into the biographical sketch accompanying a story on Joseph Argyle. Mr. Argyle cannot simultaneously whistle, stand on his head, and drink beer.

• *Apology:* I originally wrote, "Woodrow Wilson's wife grazed sheep on the front lawn of the White House." I'm sorry that typesetting inadvertently left out the word *sheep.*

Carpenter—five years' minimum experience. Quality, contentious, and hard working.

The Addles of Advertising

Economist John Kenneth Galbraith once wrote, "Few people at the beginning of the nineteenth century needed an adman to tell them what they wanted." Two centuries later, the average American reads, sees, or hears about 5,000 advertising messages a day!

And counting, of course.

It's easy to imagine all of us, in the not-too-distant future, displaying endless commercials on the electronic display boards we'll have installed in our foreheads.

The good news is that we'll always have something to do if someone is boring us.

The bad news is that we'll never be sure if someone is actually listening to us, or just watching TV.

If, however, the person whose attention we hope we have suddenly laughs when we weren't being funny at all, that'll be a pretty good indication that he has been surreptitiously viewing our foreheads. And he surely won't be able to help laughing if ever he sees the Head-O-Rama version of the following addled ads from across the country. In our ad, ad, ad, ad world, many printed examples fail to deliver added value. Instead, they offer us ad-dud value:

• Your home deserves a monthly termite inspection, so when you think of pests, think of Chuck O'Hara, your Terminex man.

• Nordic track $300. Hardly used. Call Chubby.

• Girl wanted to assist magician in cutting-off-head illusion. Benefits: Blue Cross Medical Insurance and salary.

• Psychic Dee Miller is back. Pittsburgh's most renounced psychic.

• WANTED: Meat Inspector: The successful candidate will be expected to ensure that no food fit for human consumption leaves the slaughterhouse for distribution to the general public.

• Braille dictionary for sale. Must see to appreciate.

• Our shoe stores are featuring sneakers that are ideal for streetwalking.

• Composted Horse Manure direct from the manufacturer.

• Our dental facility is one of the few offices licensed to treat you while sedated.

• On a restaurant menu: Kids. Served on White Bread.

• On a real estate site: Will build to suite.

• CHOCOLATE EGGS AND BUNNIES: Easter specialties will include hand-decorated milk and dark chocolate eggs, jelly beans, and a wicker basket with a variety of eggs and chocolate rabbis.

• My daughter developed allegories to guinea pigs. Must go. Brand-new cage negotiable.

- We have 14 riding lawn mowers for sale. We stand behind every one.
- Dental cleaning—100 percent non-painless
- Christmas tag-sale. Handmade gifts for the hard-to-find person.
- Our delivery service knows how to make a 12-piece china set arrive in 1 piece, instead of 100.
- For a hair salon: First Cut, Half Off
- House for sale: Two bedrooms, vinyl siding, well insulted. A change in family circumstances necessitates their finding a new, quiet home.
- Half Fresh Loaf of Bread
- This Saturday and Sunday: dog show. Monday: flea market
- The Bird's Nest Bed & Breakfast. Wake up to a large, delicious breakfast served in your bathrobe.
- Discover the Master's Plan for Mastering Life with Larry Loser & David Loser.
- FOR SALE: Ferret, likes kids, nice pet, but chewed the guinea pig's ear off. Also, partially deaf guinea pig.
- Bearded men and women and children (all ages) wanted for feature film.
- LOST: Male cat. Needs medication. Owner is very worried, neutered, and declawed.
- Six Donuts. Only $1.50. Limit two per customer.
- Carpenter—five years' minimum experience. Quality, contentious, and hardworking.
- USED TOMBSTONE, perfect for someone named Homer Hendel Bergen Heinzel. One only.
- Remember Mom with the Everlasting Rose. The beautiful rose, preserved in 24k Gold, is now available at just $49.00. Choose this gift for Mom or even someone you really care about.
- Single female, 27, sensitive, caring, enjoys bomb fires.
- FOR SALE: One female Hereford bull
- FOR SALE: Wedding dress and bridesmaids
- The world's newest airline is looking for the world's finest stew-

ards and stewardesses. Applicants must be over 20 years of age, single, with minimum height of 5'3" and be able to swim.

- Room and Broad—$400 a month.
- Fresh Burgers. For a limited time only.
- Auto Repair Service. Free pickup and delivery. Try us once, you'll never go anywhere again.
- Vacation Special: Have your home exterminated.
- For Rent: Six-room hated apartment.
- Man, honest. Will take anything.
- TO GIVE AWAY: One-year-old Shiatsu cross. Needs good home. Good with children and other animals.
- When you are thinking of having your next affair, remember a Holiday Inn motel.
- Duck-filled eiderdown, excellent condition
- Gardener required for part-time work: Eight hours per weed.
- After I took Impulse I started to feel myself again.
- Open House: Alzheimer's Center Prepares for an Affair to Remember.
- LOST: Deaf Golden Labrador. Doesn't answer to name "Winnie."

Here's the text of one of the cleverest ads I've ever classified:

SINGLE BLACK FEMALE: SBF Seeks male companionship, ethnicity unimportant.

I'm a svelte good-looking girl who LOVES to play. I love long walks in the woods. Riding in your pickup truck. Hunting. Camping. Fishing trips. Cozy winter nights spent lying by the fire.

Candlelight dinners will have me eating out of your hand. Rub me the right way and watch me respond! I'll be at the front door when you get home from work, wearing only what nature gave me! Kiss me and I'm yours!

Call 555-1234 and ask for Daisy

Over 15,000 men found themselves talking to the local Humane Society about an eight-week-old Labrador Retriever.

THE HALL OF FAME
OF ADS THAT DON'T AD UP

- Remember, you get what you pay for. And at Hub Furniture Store you pay less.
- We are proud of the part we have played in the tremendous growth of our city.

—Valley Mattress Company

- Don't break your back taking care of your lawn. Let us do it for you!
- Giant Stuff-a-Pumpkin Bag. Have fun stuffing this giant pumpkin with friends & family.
- Use our medicine, and you can kiss your hemorrhoids good-bye.
- LOST DOG—mixed breed, shaggy, left front leg amputated, missing top of right ear, partially blind, tail was broken and healed crooked, some teeth gone, scars on head and back, has been castrated. Answers to name of Lucky.

Lost in Translation

On an Indonesian menu: Amiable and sour pork.

The Language Barrier

ay you're munching on escargot in an outdoor café in the south of France. When the garçon asks you how your meal is, you put your thumb and forefinger together to flash him the OK sign. He storms out of the room. Why? Because in the south of France our OK hand signal means "zero, worthless."

While the curling of the forefinger and the thumb into a circle is the best-known nonvulgar hand gesture in the United States, you could end up wearing your dinner in your hair in Mexico, where it means "sex," or in Argentina, Brazil, Greece, Malta, Paraguay, Russia, Singapore, Spain, and Tunisia, where the OK sign refers to certain body parts and constitutes an insult.

So OK is not OK everywhere, OK?

Now let's place the shoe on the other foot. Here are some other cross-border translations that turn out not to be OK in English-speaking countries:

In a Japanese fashion magazine appears "JOYFUL ENGLISH LOVELY" printed beneath a cartoon of Bambi. Much of Japanese commercial English, also known as "Engrish," is English Lovely or English Charming, or English Confusing.

A T-shirt carried this actually poetic passage of English Lovely: "This wants to show the continuation of a dream for them, even if the day which bursts into flames even if it rains and a wind blows and a calm night are the ends in the world."

Where can I buy that shirt?

A Nagasaki coffee shop sports the name Placebo Labor Handbag. Other Japanese establishments display monikers such as Ghastly Custom Shops, Ox-Creation Beauty Parlor, Business Incubator, Tomato Bank, Café Feel, and Café Aspirin.

Believe it or not, there's a soup made in Japan called The Goo, a line of cosmetics named Cookie Face, rolls of toilet paper identified as Naïve Lady and My Fannie Print, and an antifreeze branded Hot Piss. Proof that the Japanese have a love affair with all things English can be seen in their signs and brand names—Great Coffee Smile, the Bathing Ape, Acid Milk, Booty Trap Jeans, Sweet Camel Jeans, Love Body, X-Box, Snatch, Catch Eye! Catalog Shopping, Ministry Candy Stripper, and Hawaiian Plucked Bread.

The ad copy for a brand of bread baked in Tokyo announces, "All of contents are no additional. It's burned to a crisp with all our heart," and an ad for a calendar heralds, "Skin clock for those wishing to become a dog." Among other Japanese ad lines we discover "Number worth plentys mean," "Happy is he who other men's charms beware,"

"A frolicking pure spiritual existence out of the blue," "No stagnant emotion," "Girl meet boys," "Violence jack off," "Look at reality, walk straight ahead," and—a typical message printed on a Japanese shopping bag—"Now baby. Tonight I am feeling cool and hard boiled."

The Japanese take on English doesn't stop there:

- *A greeting card message:* For you, I always think of your thing.
- *A hotel sign:* Come on My House.
- *Sign for rest rooms:* Go back toward your behind.
- *On a motel:* Pleasurable and gratifying rooms
- *In a restaurant window:* Please do not bring outside food, excluding children under five. Thank you.
- *In another restaurant:* Please Keep chair on position & Keep tables cleaned after dying. Thanks for your corporation.
- *In yet another restaurant:* Persons eating restaurant using cell will be eliminated.
- *In a hotel:* Maid tipping is generous for services. More is better.
- *Wake-up message from the front desk of a hotel:* Your time is up.
- *Sewerage treatment plant as marked on a Tokyo map:* Dirty Water Punishment Place
- *On a package of drinking straws:* Let's try homeparty fashionbly and have a joyful chat with nice fellow. Fujinami's straw will produce you young party happily and exceedingly!

An Indian speaker of English wrote, "Dear madam: It has been awhile since we have had intercourse. I hope you have been in good hygiene." Any implications that the Japanese have cornered the market on world-class bloopers are completely unwarranted. With all due acknowledgment of our own shortcomings when it comes to foreign tongues, here is a celebration of signs and other written English that provide an unexpected source of amusement for travelers around the world. As an ad for a Mexican English-language school promises, "Broken English spoken fluently."

• *In a St. Petersburg, Russia, brochure:* Be sure to visit Senate Square and look at the Copper Horseman, a beautiful erection of Peter the Great.

• *In a Florentine glove shop:* Our gloves can be washed in soup and water.

• *In the window of an Istanbul souvenir shop:* Sorry, we are open.

• *In a Taiwan hotel room:* Please beware of strangers dangling in the lobby.

• *Taiwanese advertisement for men's underwear:* They're comfartable!

• *Name of a store in China:* Sexual Health Thing Shop

• *Name of another Chinese store:* Warm and Fragrant Bird

• *In an African safari park:* Elephants please stay in car.

• *On an Asian charter airline:* Do not smoke when you get into the toilet. Do not throw foreign bodies in the toilet.

• *In the window of a Laundromat in Chiang Mai, Thailand:* For best results, drop pants here.

• *Name of a store in Thailand:* Pay All You Can

• *In a Mexican brochure:* Come to Juan's Jewelry Shop. We won't screw you too much.

• *In a German hotel:* Serve You Right

• *On an Indonesian menu:* Amiable and sour pork

• *In the washroom of a German train:* To obtain water, move the handle to the left or to the right, indifferently.

• *On a Chinese train:* Please do not throw yourself out the window.

• *In a Budapest zoo:* Please do not feed the animals. If you have any suitable food, give it to the guard on duty.

• *Doorway signs in the Nigerian National Theatre:* "In Entrance," "Out Entrance"

• *Ad in the Jakarta* Post: FOR RENT: Condom. Only $650 US

• *Notice in a public bathroom in Florence, the cradle of the Italian language:*

> THIS WC IS GOOF FOR EVERYONE.
> WOULD YOU LIKE TO COME BACK USING IT?
> COLLABORATE WITH EDUCATION.
> DON'T THROW BODIES SOLID INTO
> TOILETTES!
> WITH GRACIOUS THANKS,
> THE DIRECTION

THE HALL OF FAME OF GLOBAL GABBLE

- *In a Bucharest hotel lobby:* The lift is being fixed for the next day. During that time we regret that you will be unbearable.
- *In a Hong Kong supermarket:* For your convenience, we recommend courteous, efficient self-service.
- *In a Tel Aviv hotel:* If you wish for room service breakfast, lift our telephone, and the waitress will arrive. This will be enough to bring your food up.
- *In a Cairo tourist office advertising a donkey ride:* Would you like to ride on your own ass?
- *In an Acapulco restaurant:* The manager has personally passed all the water served here.

"Use repeatedly for severe damage," reads the label on a Taiwanese shampoo.

Simply Swallow Instructions

Wouldn't it be great if life came with printed instructions? "To eat, insert food into highly malleable hole directly beneath protruding odor-detection unit. Using up-and-down motion of teeth, grind food to a pulp. Using waving motion of tongue, force food down tube at back of mouth. Resist vocally communicating during this process. Repeat until satisfied. May cause drowsiness."

Or: "To walk for the first time, balance upright on chubby little baby legs. Lean forward. While flapping arms, move legs and feet in such a way as to stave off resuming of seated position. Crash back onto ground. Repeat. Squealing while upright optional."

But, of course, directions of that sort just aren't realistic. After all, babies can't read. But if they *could*, it's a sure bet they'd be just like the rest of us: they'd love printed instructions. Oh, sure, we may at times *pretend* to be indifferent about whatever instructions accompany whatever we've gotten ourselves into. "Assembling a bicycle!" we scoff. "Why, I used to ride these things all the time! How hard can it be to put one together?" Or "Honey, go ahead and put my food on the table! I'll be done assembling this entertainment unit in no time!" Or "A $25 installation charge? Ha! Just leave my dishwasher right here in the kitchen. I'll do it myself!"

But as sure as Tab A wouldn't fit into Slot B if we attacked Slot B with a chain saw, sooner or later we're apt to discover that, after all, we are at least willing to give the ol' instructions a try.

When that moment comes, we can only hope that the directives awaiting us were either written or translated very well indeed. Which is, apparently, easier said than done, just as the following are most certainly easier *read* than done:

"Not to be used for the other use," advise instructions on a Japanese blender. "Let's decompose and enjoy assembling," suggest instructions on a Taiwanese puzzle. "Use repeatedly for severe damage," reads the label on a Taiwanese shampoo.

But the best examples of lost-in-translation instructions are the longer ones. Take this disquisition for a game made in Thailand. It consists of a small wooden board, similar to that used for cribbage, and a number of pegs:

BALL BALL GAME   **FOR TWO PLAYERS.**

RACEING CROWN

The Object: Has to rancing pegs to the triancle (the winner placed) on the board. *Play:* You make bolling the dice, one at a time, to get the start one colour peg, you move

Alternately placing on the board. If you have the lost peg of the rancing

lines have many holes to capture the rancing pegs who're lost peg, you must begin at starting-point and get the start one colour peg.

After the player who're lost six same colour pegs on the poard is defeated or can be move to the triangle on the poard winner of the game.

Now that wasn't hard, was it? I'm confident that you're now ready to play the Raceing Crown game.

"Adults: One tablet three times a day until passing away," ominously direct the instructions on a Japanese medicine bottle. In the spirit of the warning labels that you'll find elsewhere in this book, the safety warnings from other countries are starkly dark.

I have in hand a set of instructions for a "Spin Top Vehicle," a miniature stunt car toy. The instructions are written in Japanese and English and include such helpful commandments for assembling as "the erection go forwards to take the contrary hour hand direction of ex-round to hover around." But the "Safe Rule" directives are the real gems of this collection—so bright and goofy that I reprint, word for word, all nine admonitions:

1. Prohibition against three years old below of child usage;
2. Play attention, you of finger, hair, clothes, etc. Don't touch and car wheel, in order to prevent quilt harm;
3. Car while driving not want to by hand grasp it;
4. Don't let the remote control close to any fire with car original, such as stove beside or mightiness of sunlight bottom;
5. Not want the place in danger to play;
6. Don't let the wet water of car, and not want under the rainy day is open-air usage;
7. Not want on the sand ground to play;

8. Forbid the child to tear open the remote control with the car;
9. If the car dash to pieces, and should pass by the per son check or profession personnel maintain the rear can continue to use.

Those instructions are rivaled by a cautionary label, translated from Korean, on an adhesive roller made for cleaning lint off clothing and upholstery:

1. Do not use this roller to the floorings that made of wood and plastic.
2. Do not use this roller to clean the stuffs that dangerous to your hands such as glass and chinaware.
3. Do not use this roller to people's heads, it is dangerous that hair could be sticked up to cause unexpected suffering.

And finally and most ominously, a small sheet of instructions that accompany a toy made in Japan. The sheet includes a drawing of a skull and crossbones:

DANGER! A dangerous toy. This toy is being made for the extreme property the good looks. This little part which suffocated when the sharp part which gets hurt is swallowed is contained generously. Only the person who can take responsibility by itself is to play.

THE HALL OF FAME OF FOREIGN MENUS

- *On a Swiss menu:* Our wines leave you nothing to hope for.
- *On a Shanghai Mongolian hot pot menu:* You will be able to eat all you wish until you are fed up.
- *On another Chinese menu:* Special cocktails for women with nuts.
- *On yet another Chinese menu:* Mr. Zheng and his fellowworkers like to meet you and entertain you with their hostility and unique cooking techniques.
- *On an Indian menu:* Our establishment serves tea in a bag like mother.

English: "It takes a tough man
to make a tender chicken."

Spanish: "It takes a sexually
excited man to make a
chicken affectionate."

Brand Slams

We hear much these days about the Global Economy, about how every day the world grows smaller, in that every day people around the world want to buy the same things. It's one thing when, say, American diplomats visit a remote Asian or Middle Eastern country; it's another altogether when Britney Spears or the house that Ronald McDonald built starts showing up on every corner. What exciting times these must be for those working in international product marketing and advertising! How exciting it must be to hold in your hands a product you just *know* is going to find its way into the lives of people so distant from you it's impossible to imagine their weather, much less what they're planning to buy this month.

How thrilling to know that, before too very long, they'll be buying whatever you're selling!

Is it any wonder companies so often rush to introduce their products into foreign markets? Think of the social implications! Think of the cultural cross-fertilization! Think of the inevitably liberating impact of a free, open-market economy!

Think of the cash!

The key word is "think." And that's something everyone involved with bringing a product to a foreign market should do lots and lots of before doing anything irrevocable. Because while everyone may speak the universal language of commerce, there are still about 200 other languages out there with a million or more native speakers. And that means that while Britney Spears and Ronald McDonald might be welcomed in some markets, their translated incarnations—"British Stabbing Stick" and "Red-Nosed Meat Clown," say—might find a cooler reception in others.

That's the nature of language: what seems like a surefire marketing strategy in one language may get you run out of a town with a different culture. Sometimes—and especially when it comes to international business—it's the *seller* who must beware:

• The Osco Company bought out Sav-On Drugs and planned to change all the store names to Osco. Finally, they discovered that in Mexican Spanish *osco* is slang for feeling sick.

• Commodore renamed its VIC line of personal computers VC in German-speaking areas. Why? Because "Fick," which is how "VIC" would be pronounced, is a vulgar verb in German.

• Powergen, a British electricity company, bought an electricity company in Italy. Its original Web site name was www.powergenitalia.

• Mensa, the name of the international high-IQ society, means "stupid" in Spanish.

The best-laid plans of mice and men and marketers go awry when clever slogans in English get lost in translation:

Adolph Coors:
English: "Turn it loose!"   *Spanish:* "Suffer from diarrhea!"

American Airlines:
English: "Fly in leather."   *Spanish:* "Fly naked."

Kentucky Fried Chicken:
English: "Finger-lickin' good"   *Chinese:* "Eat your fingers off."

Mars Candy:
English: "They taste like paradise."   *Hungarian:* "They taste like tomato."

Otis Elevator:
English: "Completion equipment"   *Russian:* "Equipment for orgasm"

Parker Pen:
English: "Avoid embarrassment."   *Spanish:* "Avoid pregnancy."

Pepsi-Cola:
English: "Come alive with the Pepsi generation!"   *Chinese:* "Pepsi brings back your dead ancestors!"

Perdue Farms:

English: "It takes a tough man to make a tender chicken."

Spanish: "It takes a sexually excited man to make a chicken affectionate."

3M:

English: "It sticks like crazy."

Japanese: "It sticks foolishly."

As the story goes, a disappointed salesman of soft drinks returns from his Middle East assignment. The boss calls him into office and demands, "Why wasn't your campaign successful with the Arabs?"

The salesman explains, "When I got posted to the Middle East, I was very confident I would succeed with a good sales pitch as our product is virtually unknown there. But I had a problem—I didn't know how to speak Arabic. So, I planned to convey the message through a poster with three panels."

"That sounds reasonable," the boss admits.

"The first panel showed a man crawling through the hot desert sand, totally exhausted and panting. Second, the man is drinking a big cold bottle of our cola, and the third panel showed the man again, now totally refreshed."

"Good logic," agrees the boss.

"Then I had these posters pasted all over the place."

"That should have worked," says his boss. "What happened?"

The salesman replies, "Well, not only did I not speak Arabic. I also didn't understand that Arabs read from right to left."

THE HALL OF FAME
OF BRAND SLAM BLOOPERS

As the story above illustrates, even an inapt nonverbal cue can play hob with a product's reception in a far-off land:

- Gerber's baby food initially packaged its African product the same way as in the United States—with a cute baby picture on each jar. The marketers didn't realize that because so many Africans cannot read, nearly all packaged products sold in Africa carry pictures of what's inside. Pureed baby—horrors!

- Muslims in Bangladesh rioted and ransacked Thom McAn stores when they mistook the company's logo on some sandals for the Arabic letters that spell "Allah." One person was killed and 50 people were injured before the melee ended.

Eh, What's That
You Say?

I think I'll send her flowers. That would be a nice jester.

A Mangling
of Malapropisms

Lead the way," said Mrs. Malaprop in Richard Brinsley Sheridan's play *The Rivals*, written more than two centuries ago, "and we'll precede." Of course, she meant *proceed*, but she made so many hilarious, precarious mistakes in speech that she bequeathed a new word to the language—*malapropism* the unintentionally humorous misuse of a word. Mrs. Malaprop took special pride in her use of the King's English: "Sure, if I reprehend anything in this world, it is the use of my oracular tongue and a nice derangement of epitaphs." As a result of such malapropisms, Mrs. Malaprop has become the very pineapple of word abusage, the fountain pen of linguistic humor.

The joy of language is that it allows you to express yourself. All those wonderful words to choose from! And sometimes, reaching out for just that right word, you grab one that looks and sounds like the one you're after—but, alas, it isn't.

A high-school journalism teacher assigned her student to write an article on the calligraphy that was decorating the school rest rooms. The young man, wanting to decry the "defacement" of the school walls, wrote an entire article on the "defecation" of the school walls. Lucky that the newspaper didn't get sued for defecation of character.

On that same subject—and by a process of elimination—Lawrence Spivak, while interviewing astronaut Wally Schirra, asked, "How does it feel to be in a state of wastelessness?"

When a high-powered agent of the company walked into the lunchroom, a secretary remarked that she couldn't stand him because he was so "ego-testicle." The listeners spat coffee out of their noses.

"Do You Ever Spit?" led off a magazine article. "Three out of every five of us have from time to time been known to expurgate on public streets, with men almost twice as likely as women to do so." Great expectorations!

As Mark Twain explained, "The difference between the almost right word and the right word is really a large matter—'tis the difference between the lightning-bug and the lightning." Have a look at a collection of de-light-ful lightning bugs that run the full gauntlet from alfalfa to omega:

- Eight candidates, including all four incompetents, are seeking the four City Council positions this year.
- Mrs. Brown is visiting her sister, Mrs. Jackson, who is ill with an absence in her head.
- We currently show 82 returned e-mails between 10:28 A.M. and 1:39 P.M. today. . . . We have sent an inquiry to determine if, due to congesting, this is a temporary condition. We apologize for any incontinence this may cause.

- *On a statement of credit card benefits:* There is no coverage for claims due to fraud, abuse, vermin, war, or hostilities of any kind, for example, invasion, rebellion, or resurrection.
- A score of informal cocktail parties preceded the Press Club dinner. An improper desert party followed.
- Troops were up for revelry at 5:30 A.M.
- Whatever happened to the separation of Church and state? Look what they're displaying at the state capitol building during Christmas—a scene of the activity!
- Newburger said the GSA chief, David J. Barram, would wait for a winner apparent to the entire electorate before exercising his desecration to release federal transition funds.
- *Conditions that allow a visit to the emergency room:* Heart attack, severe bleeding, and loss of conscience.
- Missouri, where the mountain lion was hunted to distinction by 1927, has confirmed its fifth citing of a mountain lion in a decade.
- Dear Abby: My mother is mean and short-tempered. I think she is going through her mental pause.
- An argument erupted between two patrons at a Hardee's restaurant and ended up with two deaths. But D'Addario says it would have been worse if not for the restaurant's manager. "When the first epitaph was spoken, our manager tried to settle the affair, and when that didn't work, he rounded up all his employees so none of them would get hurt," the security chief said.
- Vandals struck early Tuesday morning, spray-painting racist, anti-Semantic, and antipolice slurs on two town vehicles and other cars near the Donald R. Marquis Minuteman Trail.
- We've spotted one regular customer of this drugstore who is constantly shoplifting. She's a real nymphomaniac.
- He's very clever with his puns and playing with words, especially when he tosses off a double nintendo.
- There are already too few beds at the mission. Something that increases homelessness will only exasperate the situation.
- There were a lot of old-timers still around who are important clogs in the commission machinery.

- My daughter and her husband bought a great house. It's safe for the kids, too. It's on a cutty sark.
- Read and be aware of these virus problems. They can play haddock with your database and family lines.
- A prominent Los Angeles lawyer who specialized in labor and litigation matters died reluctantly on March 22.
- The bride walked up the aisle. On her neck she wore a cross necklace. On his head, the groom wore a Yamaha.
- What if someone in your household called this number? Would there be negative percussions?
- His candidacy was a flash in the pants.
- My sister has extra-century perception.
- It's a catch 20-20 situation.
- Sam Walton is as rich as crocuses.
- She was greeted with a standing ovulation.
- As far as I'm concerned, it's a mute question.
- I'm not sure that they should have passed the mustard.
- Nobody is diluting themselves that you are going to pull it off.
- We have to look at each side of this many-fauceted problem.
- The best strategy for peace is a nuclear detergent.
- Partly cloudy with a chance of intimate showers.
- My son bats lefty and throws righty. He's amphibian.
- That's not a fact. It's only suppository.
- Live Flamingo Spanish Music.
- There's no reason to get into a state of high dungeon.
- I'm going to have to take a night flight to Philadelphia. I hate flying deadeye.
- The evidence is incontroversial.
- We are going to sing today without musical accompaniment, or Acapulco.
- Firefighters arrived at the scene and distinguished the blaze.
- A brother can't marry his sister. That would be incesticide.
- I want to be a ball bearing at your funeral.
- He's nothing but a liar and a prefabricator.

- I described it in lame man's terms.
- Relaxation is not a placenta for everything.
- Rusty Banazek broke his clavichord in scrimmage.
- I am a vociferous reader.
- All the kids in the neighborhood were conjugating on the corner.
- There's a great deal of skull-drudgery going on.
- Go down Laskey Road. It runs paranoid to Alexis.
- There was a big fire, and they had to vacuum a lot of people from the building.
- They say she has a photogenic memory.
- Before becoming a saint, one has to be beautified.
- The family lives way out in the boondoggles.
- The story is made up, so the names of all the characters are facetious.
- He's a war mongrel.
- Unless dues are paid by March 1, you will be dismembered.
- Smoking cigarettes will stump your growth.
- I think I'll send her flowers. That would be a nice jester.
- I drank way too much last night; I was completely obliviated.
- There he sat, smiling like a cheddar cat.
- The *Philadelphia Inquirer*, in a roundup of the year's events, gave its "Latin Prize" to a local TV newswoman. She reportedly had called the district attorney's office to ask how to get to "Absentia," where, she had heard, a murder trial was being held.

- Ortiz is the most recent recipient of the pretentious Con Edison Athlete of the Week Award.
- The cookbook is being compiled. Please submit your favorite recipe and a short antidote concerning it.
- At the university, three classes of professors compromise the teaching staff.
- Persons interested in using my secretary's reproductive equipment should contact me first.
- Senators are chosen as committee chairmen on the basis of senility.
- When shipping fragile items, I always pack the box with xylophones.

He came through the experience smelling like a knight in shining armor.

A Mixing of Metaphors

Chances are you've very recently used a metaphor. Just try communicating without employing a figure of speech or two. It's like walking with your feet chained together or fighting with one hand tied behind your back. See? Metaphors are impossible to avoid. They pop up like daisies on a cow patty.

Of course, nobody says that all metaphors have to be deathless prose. But those that are—or at least those that have stood the test of time—are as much a part of our language as nouns, verbs, slang, and . . . pregnant pauses.

"We were packed in there like sardines."

"That's a real feather in your cap."

"These days everyone's feeling the pinch."

"The project is shrouded in a cloak of secrecy."

"When I'm busy as a beaver and a bee, I'm happy as a clam and a lark."

See? We use metaphors all the time. They're the cat's pajamas and the cat's meow (phrases that haven't stood the test of time). They help us break the ice, bury the hatchet, blow off steam, and raise the bar for what makes colorful language. Without metaphors, we'd be out in left field and up the creek without a paddle. When it comes to effective communication, Metaphors Be With You!

Unfortunately, the strength of the metaphor is also its weakness. Because they're used so often—and because so many of them sound or seem so much alike—it's easy to accidentally jumble two of them together, even when you *aren't* a bubble off plumb and three sheets to the wind. Flying in the face of physics, two metaphors *can* occupy the same space at the same time.

Should you ever realize that you've promiscuously mixed your metaphors, don't feel as if you've laid an egg, or have egg on your face, or that you're walking on eggshells, or are sucking eggs. Don't feel that you need to eat crow or humble pie—or humble crow, for that matter. After all, sometimes that's just the way the cookie crumbles, as we see when metaphors collide:

• It's easy to sympathize with Bush. He must be enormously frustrated to see President Clinton as mired in the limelight as a Goodyear Blimp lodged in the Lincoln Tunnel.

• We are in a butt-ugly recession right now, but we are seeing light at the end of the tunnel.

• It is only a snake in the grass who will attempt to knife a man in the back with so evil-smelling a report.

- But within two days of getting the projects off the ground, we were told they would have to be frozen. This latest attempt to relieve some of the pressure is welcome, but still leaves a vacuum of discontent.

- Adam Poncho, Arroyo's attorney, said Arroyo has offered to help Arias, who is diabetic and had one leg amputated. "She's offered to buy him an artificial leg, no strings attached," Poncho said.

- Traditional music is music handed down by ear.

- *A Pentagon staffer, complaining that efforts to reform the military have thus far been too timid:* "It's just ham-fisted salami-slicing by the bean counters."

- In a report on attempts by pharmaceutical companies to create a version of Viagra for women, a clinical psychologist commented, "The idea that there is some normal level of sexual functioning drives me up the creek."

- We traveled through remote Chinese villages where the hand of Westerners has never set foot.

- It is the opinion of many observers that in handling the situation, the president hit the bull's-eye on the nose.

- I don't think it helps people to start throwing white elephants and red herrings at each other.

- The media report violent events, which leads others to become violent. That leads to more reporting, which brings on still more violence. It's a vicious snowball.

- You can lead a horse to the water, but you can't look in his mouth.

- This is not rocket surgery, you know.

- He turned a blind ear to that issue.

- That's his crutch to bear.

- Come on. Let's cut to the mustard.

- My mother literally worked like a Trojan horse to put me through college.

- You must put your foot down with a firm hand.

- He minced no bones in talking about civil rights.

- They pulled the plug out from under me.
- The politicians are jumping through loopholes.
- It's like beating the horse after the barn door has been closed.
- You threw me for a curve.
- Fish or get off the pot.
- Don't worry; I've got an ace up my hole.
- The idea came like a bolt out of a bat.
- The grass is always greener on the other side of the tracks.
- We are going to be shooting from the seat of our pants on this one.
- Let's jump off that bridge when we come to it.
- I can see through you like a book.
- He came through the experience smelling like a knight in shining armor.
- Your Honor, when I vacated that apartment, it was as clean as the nose on my face.
- Don't put all your chickens in one basket.
- Oh, that's just so much water over the bridge.
- I'm not going to get sidetracked onto a tangent.
- Now the shoe is on the horse of a different color.
- You're talking through the skin of your teeth.
- Call a family meeting and get all the dirty dishwater ironed out once and forever.
- As far as my writing career goes, this project could be the gravy on the cake.
- He took me under his coattails.
- I had the world by the oyster.

So let's grab the bull by the tail and look it directly in the eye. When you boil it right down to brass tacks (a specimen cited by linguist Bergen Evans), it is best to avoid mixing your metaphors.

THE HALL OF FAME
OF MIXED METAPHORS

- The bankers' pockets are bulging with the sweat of the honest workingman.
- The sacred cows have come home to roost with a vengeance.
- I have a mind like a steel sieve.
- She was a diva of such immense talent that, after she performed, there was seldom a dry seat in the house.
- We have buttered our bread, and now we have to sleep in it.
- They're biting the hand of the goose that laid the golden egg.

—Samuel Goldwyn

Illegal income, such as stolen or embezzled funds, must be included in your gross income on line 21 of Form 1040 or on Schedule C-EZ.

Fuzzy Logic

Eugene Ormandy, longtime conductor of the Philadelphia orchestra, was known for making statements that were a bubble off plumb and a french fry short of a Happy Meal:

- Glen Miller became a legend in his own lifetime due to his early death.
- Who is sitting in that empty chair?
- Thank you for your cooperation and vice versa.
- That was perfect. It was just the opposite from what I said yesterday.

- Bizet was a very young man when he composed this symphony, so play it softly.
- He's a good man—and so is his wife.
- This is a very democratic organization, so let's take a vote. All those who disagree with me, raise their hands.

The case of the great conductor illustrates an important truth: fame offers no vaccine against a brilliant mind or famous face tripping over its own words as stepping on its own tongue:

- I am grateful to all the fans, and especially God.

    —*Janet Jackson at the* Billboard *Music Awards*

- We've got to pause and ask ourselves: how much clean air do we need?

    —*Lee Iacocca*

- It was not my class of people. There was not a producer, a press agent, a director, an actor.

    —*Zsa Zsa Gabor, on the jury used in her assault trial*

- It doesn't matter if you're rich or poor, as long as you've got money.

    —*Joe E. Lewis*

- And now the sequence of events in no particular order.

    —*Dan Rather, CBS television news anchor*

These luminaries are joined by us ordinary people. Some of us are born stupid. Others achieve stupidity. Some have stupidity thrust upon them:

- As of tomorrow, employees will only be able to access the building using individual security cards. Pictures will be taken next Wednesday, and employees will receive their cards in two weeks.

- All employees are invited to the annual Christmas party. All children under the age of ten will receive a gift from Santa. Employees who have no children may bring grandchildren.
- Incredibly, Lou Gehrig himself actually died of Lou Gehrig's disease. Isn't that something?
- Of course you don't remember the first time you heard that song; you weren't even born yet!
- Nine youngsters were playing with a stray dog in a field near Rolling Prairie when the dog dug up $587 in currency. The children turned the money over to the sheriff, but no one claimed it, so the sheriff divided it among the nine children. He added a little of his own, and they got $60 apiece.
- The Lancaster City Health Department announced today that due to the increased demand for birth and death certificates, they must be ordered at least one week in advance.
- Five presidents, with the exception of James Buchanan, who was a bachelor, were childless.
- Although this is mainly a diversity fair, all are welcome.
- Statistics show that teenage pregnancies drop off significantly after age 25.
- Because of the dreadful crimes of which unregenerate man is capable, the death penalty should be there to emphasize the sanctity of human life and protect it.
- *Instructions posted in a river cruise ship:* The chairs in the cabin are for the ladies. Gentlemen are not to make use of them till the ladies are seated.
- Some 40 percent of female gas station employees in Metro Detroit are women, up from almost none a year ago.
- Young ladies between 15 and 71 required.
- The decline in the birth rate has caused a substantial drop in the number of babies born each year.
- Never forget the power of understatement. It is the greatest unused force in advertising!
- New Brunswick has been selected as the pilot province for what could become a national "numeracy" campaign. The Canadian

Bankers Association selected this province because of its recent success with literacy, which has been reduced from 23.9 to 19.5 percent.

- Ramos is the mother of two grown sons and two grandchildren.
- His music is more contemporary today than it was a few years ago.
- My father has developed, in his late nineties, a congenital heart disease.
- I didn't know "Onward Christian Soldiers" was a Christian song.
- *From California driver handbook instructions:* Your thumb or fingerprint will be taken.
- Cardiac arrest is still rare under age 35, accounting for just 1 percent of all deaths resulting from it.
- Patients spend 10 to 16 weeks in the hospital from the time they are diagnosed to the time they die. We must get this down to 7 to 10 days. Practice nurses can make it happen.
- The program will be televised live about one hour after the event.
- The element of surprise caught us totally off guard.
- Please leave no milk today. When I say today, I mean tomorrow, for I wrote this note yesterday.

> CABARET SHOWTIME
> PRESENTING ACAPELLA GROUP
> THE PLAIDS
> ACCOMPANIED BY THE GALAXY ORCHESTRA

- Fish and Wildlife Services scientists plan to kill about 40 stocky black sea ducks called surf scooters around Commencement Bay to find out why their numbers are declining.
- Collene Campbell champions the rights of murder victims after being one herself more than once.

- The trouble with Harbor Island is that it's overrun by absentee landlords.
- He has never done anything like that, and he won't ever do it again.
- *On an expressway construction area:* Permitted Loads Not Permitted
- *At the bottom of a receipt for funeral arrangements:* Thank you. Please come again.
- Miss Giavollela had pleaded guilty to taking goods from Tesco Supermarket, to assaulting a policewoman, and to dishonestly handling a garden gnome.
- I stayed awake last night dreaming about you.

—character on Secret Storm

- I have a wife and three kids, all under 12 years old.

—victim on Dragnet

- Nearly two-thirds of African-American children were born out of wedlock in 2001.
- *An advertisement in an Eau Claire, Wisconsin, newsletter:* When applying to a blind box ad, please indicate the names of the companies you do not want us to forward your résumé to. Your résumé will then be discarded.
- *From a U.K. Department of Health and Social Services explanation regarding mobility allowances for the disabled:* A person shall not be treated as suffering from physical disablement such that he is either unable to walk or virtually unable to do so if he is not unable to or virtually unable to walk with a prosthesis or an artificial aid which he habitually wears or if he would not be unable or virtually unable to walk if he habitually wore or used a prosthesis or an artificial aid which is suitable in his case.
- *From an Internal Revenue Service publication:* Illegal income, such as stolen or embezzled funds, must be included in your gross income on line 21 of Form 1040 or on Schedule C-EZ.
- *On a radio station:* After this announcement, we will continue with our uninterrupted music.

- To get to our store, take 58 East, exit at first Tehachapie exit, turn right, and go straight through two turn signals and two stop signs:

- *Spoken by a Los Angeles radio DJ shortly after the 1990 earthquake:* The telephone company is urging people to please not use the telephone unless it is absolutely necessary in order to keep the lines open for emergency personnel. We'll be right back after this break to give away a pair of Phil Collins concert tickets to caller number 95.

THE HALL OF FAME
OF ILLOGICAL LOGIC

- If I had known I was going to live this long, I'd have taken better care of myself.

  —jazz musician Eubie Blake, who smoked from the age of six and never drank water—on his hundredth birthday

- Please accept my resignation. I don't want to belong to any club that will have me as a member.

  —Groucho Marx

- It's not that I'm afraid to die. I just don't want to be there when it happens.

  —Woody Allen

- I can resist anything but temptation.

  —Oscar Wilde

- Anybody who goes to a psychiatrist ought to have his head examined.

  —Samuel Goldwyn

A new toy Yoda

Casting a Spell

ot long ago, a former waitress was made the victim of a linguistic hoax. Jodee Berry, 26, of Panama City, said in a lawsuit that a new Hooters Restaurant boss reneged on his promise to give her a "new Toyota."

Ms. Berry says she was a waitress during the spring when the Panama City Beach Hooters manager, Jared Blair, announced a contest to promote beer sales. Berry said Blair told the waitresses that the company would reward the one who sold the most beer during April. According to the plaintiff, Blair said that the contest was a regional promotion, and that the top ten waitresses from each restaurant would be entered in a drawing.

"I couldn't believe that out of all the girls who were entered, I was the winner," Berry said. She was blindfolded and led to the restaurant's parking lot, she said. When the blindfold was removed, according to the lawsuit, Berry didn't see a new car. Instead, she gazed at a new toy Yoda, the little green, pointy-eared guy from the *Star Wars* movies.

Berry said she looked beyond the $40 Yoda hoping to see the car driving around the corner. When the car failed to appear, she realized the toy was her prize. The manager stayed in the restaurant laughing.

Jodee Berry was not amused. She sued Hooters for compensation for the cost of a new Toyota, the model to be determined, and for interest and attorney's fees. I'm pleased to report that Jodee Berry won her lawsuit.

In addition to a lesson in business ethics, that news story demonstrates that it's not always easy to figure out how a word is spelled from the way that word sounds.

A news story reported that "South Korean police officers used ropes to repel a building and arrest students." The cops must have been unsuccessful, for the building didn't back off.

On the domestic front, an analyst predicted that Florida gubernatorial candidate "Jeb Bush would win reelection by a hare's breath." That's because of Bush's rabbit fans.

A sports story quoted a coach as saying, "There's the principle of sewing and reaping. You reap what you sew if you don't get weary of doing the right things. We're starting to reap what we sew." I predict that the team will also sow up the conference title.

Another sports story informed readers, "The San Diego Chicken has transcended his character into a virtual folk hero who wonderfully fills the jester's roll." Sounds like a very large chicken sandwich.

In the policies-and-procedures manual of an on-line pharmacy portal site appears this explanation: "We are required by law to post the pharmacy's number on the medication vile in case the customer has questions about their drug use." That's some of the vilest spelling I've ever seen.

English often casts a spell over the spell-bound people who try to capture it in writing:

- The atomic time clock is a device by which we are able to determine the ages of objects up to 20,000 years old. Now it will be possible to determine the age of the mommies in Egypt.
- To make a delicious rabbit stew, use four diced carrots, one large onion, six medium-sized potatoes, and one large hair.
- She is known for her ability to work hormoneously with others.
- How was President Ronald Reagan able to resolve that situation with such self-deprecation and a plum?
- The island is a favorite spot of picneckers.
- The young blonde actress bares a striking resemblance to her famous mother.
- It always has seemed to me that death must be the most exiting of all adventures.
- As a child, Strom Thurmond lived the life of Riley in South Carolina, with butlers, groundskeepers, and maids at his beckon call.
- Executive Chef prepares his signature meal, including Duck Galantine with Veal Mouse.
- I heard that if you play "Stairway to Heaven" backwards, it says something about Satin.
- The invitation to the party says the dress is casual sheik.
- Collage is a waist of time.
- Once I opened the door to the room, she was in my arms, legs around my waste.
- The community I came from wasn't very structured, but it helled together.
- Stronghold Castle was built by William Strong, who was a big whig with the *Chicago Tribune* in the 1920s.
- The driver of the car was cited for wreckless driving.

- Ethan Frome and Mattie Silver took a slay ride.
- Passengers may stand by the rail and watch their ship being raised by a series of ingenuous locks.
- The soup at Pied de Cochon, an all-night brassiere in the Les Halles food market area, is slow-roasted in butter and white wine.
- The autopsy revealed that Kevin had died from a heroine overdose.
- She gave lessons in garment pattern drafting and dress designing and designed a foot warmer, for which she received a patient.
- This magnificent structure was destroyed during the post–World War II madness that griped Cheyenne, during which time many of Cheyenne's historic buildings were demolished.
- *At a posh hotel:* Rose pedals at turndown.
- I want to be a foreign exchange student because I would enjoy studding all over Europe.
- FOR SALE: Four rolls bedroom wallpaper, plus attractive boarder
- FOR SALE: Well-manored German shepherd
- *On a Junior ROTC Web site:* We Strive for Perfection, but We Except Excellence.
- Provide an edited, spell-checked, and grammatically corrected final version of your book on disk or through our file upload utility. You may also have our in-house editor proff your work for spelling and grammer.
- Judging of the essays will be based on spelling, punctuation, and grammaticak correctness.

- On Thanksgiving morning we could smell the foul cooking.
- Vestal virgins were pure and chased.
- Ever since the collapse of the Soviet Union, there has been a considerable decline in the value of the rubble.
- In midevil times most people were alliterate.
- Now Hillary Rodham Clinton has returned, a kinder, gentler First Lady, her tarnished halo residing over her well-coffered head.
- Mr. and Mrs. Garth Robinson request the honor of your presents at the wedding of their daughter Holly to James Stockman.

Before a captively bred bird can be released into the wild, it must pass a test:
it must be able to kill and feed itself.

Extra-Tasty
Grammar Crackers

An abstract noun," the teacher said, "is something you can think of,
but you can't touch it. Can you give me an example of one?"

"Sure," a teenage boy replied. "My father's new car."

In a Victoria Holt novel titled *The Curse of the Kings* appears this
passage: "I shall never forget the inn in the little moorland village.
The sign creaking just outside our window—a gabled one, for the inn
was three hundred years old; the sound of the waterfall less than half

a mile away sending its sparkling water over the craggy boulders and the big feather bed in which we lay together."

All of these statements, and the ones that follow, have been raided by the grammar gremlins. These little pests are the mischievous elves that sneak up on a sentence and relocate a modifier, dangle a participle, insinuate an ambiguous pronoun, yoke together two elements in some absurd way, and in general wreak havoc on the infrastructure of the prose:

- George Grant is the proud possessor of a brand-new Chevrolet sedan and also a new wife, having traded the old one for a liberal allowance.

- Walter Whitworth, who recently sold his business interests in Hartford, together with his family, returned this week to his farm near Cromwell.

- Mrs. Homer Cotton discovered a berry bush bearing both purple and red raspberries. And Mrs. Stanley Palmer—to mention another freak of nature—has an apple tree with apples and also blossoms and buds.

- *On a Halloween bag:* Children should have their parents look at their Halloween treats before eating them.

- He has since made several circumnavigations and two Pacific crossings (1989 and 1996) aboard sloops built of recycled aluminum cans, one of which was only nine-and-a-half feet long.

- By order of the selectmen, cows grazing by the roadside or riding bicycles is hereby forbidden.

- All persons caught running a car under 16 years of age, or a person running a car drunk, will be prosecuted.

- The dinner is to honor residents and interns who are leaving the hospital and their wives.

- The suspect swallowed a cyanide pill hidden in his clothing while police grilled him and slipped into a coma.

- Police said the three men got into an argument but had no information as to what they fought about.

- You can reserve your copy of the Entertainment book by calling Denise or Marjorie. They will be available for pickup in September.

- Wrap poison bottles in sandpaper and fasten with Scotch tape or a rubber band. If there are children in the house, lock them in a small metal box.

- The first thing he did was rescue Lucy Garrett's dog, and he promptly fell in love with her.

- Please send me a form for cheap milk, for I have a baby two months old and did not know about it until a neighbor told me.

- He was found unconscious by a neighbor who smelled gas and two maintenance men.

- A small jet hit an elk as it was taking off in Warrenton and caught fire.

- Dostoevsky's opinions stemmed largely from his experience as a young boy, when his father's serfs murdered him.

- Return this certificate to the Salvation Army with your gift and the reply form below to help provide toys for hurting children in San Diego County.

- The May 30 issue featured a cover photo and pictures inside of Catherine Deneuve and actress Chiara Mastoianni, 24.

- Double closets in the foyer provide plenty of space to hang your coats and guests.

- *From a TV listing:* 7 (CBS) *60 Minutes:* An school system fails to teach.

- The helmet probably saved him from more injuries when his head hit the pavement, and then came flying off.

- There will be no special shoot for the seniors, as they have been largely unsuccessful in the past.

- Voters will be staying away from the polls because of complete lack of interest and apathy.

- Please give this catalog to a friend if you already have one.

- *Answering machine message:* Please leave your disease after the tone, and the doctor will return it as soon as possible.

• The basis for Checki's lawsuit occurred on December 4, 1982, when he was a passenger in a car traveling on Interstate 10 from New Orleans to Baton Rouge. Checki observed what appeared to be an Oldsmobile rapidly approaching the rear of his car. Inside that automobile were two men wearing cowboy hats and a woman.

• The driver had a narrow escape, as a broken board penetrated his cabin and just missed his head. This had to be removed before he could be released.

• *Sign in a restaurant rest room:* Employees must wash your hands.

• Sorry not to have paid your bill before, but my wife had a baby, and I've been carrying it around in my pocket for weeks.

• Thank you in advance for helping children stricken with cancer and their families.

• By the time World War II was raging, poor eyesight and age kept the U.S. Army from accepting Mr. Schrage.

• I remember I once went on a rafting trip down the Rio Grande with the man who was then my husband and a friend of ours.

• Born to unwed parents, Wendy's Dave Thomas was adopted at six weeks. At five, his mother died.

• Before a captively bred bird is released into the wild, it must pass a test: it must be able to kill and feed itself.

• Four decades ago, the opposition to the civil right to vote was easy to identify: night riders wearing white sheets and burning crosses.

• Wealthy families hired private coaches to hone boys' athletic skills and accompany them to the Olympics. Athletes competed in the nude, and married women were barred from viewing the games, which lasted almost 1,200 years.

• *Photo caption:* Reed Beaupre, owner of Big Daddy Bagels, carries uncooked bagels to the boiling tank before being baked in the bagel shop at the Meadowbrook Shopping Center.

Even a gratuitous mark of punctuation can generate an unintended meaning. Note the effect of the missing period and capital letter in this ad: "Two eight-year-old female tortoise shells, both spayed and declawed inside cats."

Note the havoc wreaked by a missing apostrophe in this ad: "WANTED: Guitar for college student to learn to play, classical non-electric, also piano to replace daughters lost in fire."

Note the startling result of the absence of hyphens in this headline: FATHER TO BE STABBED TO DEATH IN STREET.

If you ever need an exhibit to bolster your argument for use of the serial comma—the one that's inserted before *and*, as in "red, white, and blue"—simply turn to the following book dedication: "To my parents, Ayn Rand and God."

And here's a sentence from a Realtor's pamphlet, in which a single unneeded apostrophe communicates quite a different meaning from what the author intended: "We always get our seller's top dollar."

THE UNGRAMMATICAL HALL OF FAME

- When Lady Caruthers smashed the traditional bottle of champagne against the hull of the giant oil tanker, she slipped down the runway, gained speed, rocketed into the water with a gigantic spray, and continued unchecked toward Prince's Island.
- Lady Macbeth tries to convince Macbeth to kill the king by attacking his manhood.
- During the summer, my sister and I milked the cows, but now my father milks the cows in the morning and us at night.
- Females should have the same athletic opportunities as males. It is an almost universal medical opinion that there is no sport more dangerous to a girl than a boy.
- These postcards were donated by Helen Huber, on behalf of her great-uncle, Gerhard Huber, who perished in the *Titanic* disaster and had been in a steamer trunk for 30 years.

We have been encouraging people to drive to the gym, change clothes, and work out for 20 years.

A Misplacement of Modifiers

"We spent most of our time sitting on the back porch watching the cows playing Scrabble and reading," writes a student. But just a second: It's the people who were "playing Scrabble and reading," not the cows. The modifying phrase is misplaced.

"In *The Valley Between* a prim teacher flees from a runaway bull clad only in his underwear," a book review informs us. But who is "clad only in his underwear"—the teacher or the bull? Presumably it's the teacher, but because the phrase "clad only in his underwear" comes at the end of the sentence, the reader gets the impression that it is the bull who is running around in his Skivvies.

On the *Today* show for January 15, 2002, Katie Couric said as she introduced a segment about accused spy Wen Ho Lee: "He's speaking out today for the first time since being incarcerated on the *Today* show." Where on the *Today* set did they lock up Mr. Lee?

In his classic *Modern English Usage,* grammar icon H. W. Fowler offers examples of what happens when one's modifiers go south—or north or anywhere too far away from the words they are supposed to modify: "Ask the Minster of Agriculture if he will require eggs to be stamped with the date on which they were laid by the farmer." The more modern *AP Press Guide to News Writing* advises: "The language has many ways to trip you up, most deviously through a modifier that turns up in the wrong place. Don't let related ideas in a sentence drift apart. Modifiers should be close to the word they purport to modify." Here's what happens when that fails to happen:

- With his tail held high, my father led his prize bull around the arena.
- Aided by a thousand eyes, the author explains how ants navigate and how they use dead reckoning.
- The dog was hungry and made the mistake of nipping a two-year-old that was trying to force-feed it in his ear.
- The family lawyer will read the will tomorrow at the residence of Mr. Hannon, who died June 19 to accommodate his relatives.
- The unfortunate woman was killed while cooking her husband's breakfast in a horrible manner.
- He has already been convicted of killing his wife twice.
- "He was an engaging small dog," said an observer with a curly tail and a friendly manner.
- I saw the dead dog driving down the highway.
- After months of suspicious activity, police finally raided the compound.

- Police hope an autopsy will confirm the identity of a teenage boy whose body they found stuffed into a septic tank with the help of a self-proclaimed clairvoyant.

- *Cold cases:* Nancy Lee Arnold, a food service worker, was found strangled in her Telegraph Street apartment by the manager on January 8, 1983. No suspect was ever found.

- Burgoine and Navarez have been charged with murder and assault by a grand jury.

- We will show you how to fix up your home and then sell it, for just a few dollars.

- We are threatening to relinquish the position of leadership we have held since World War I, when George Bush invaded Iraq.

- Any person purchasing tobacco products under the age of 21 must show ID every time.

- Attorney G. Clinton Gaston and Nicole Tate, one of the women named in the civil suit against the Chicago Police Department, explain the gruesome accounts of what she encountered during a *Chicago Defender* interview.

- A former St. Cloud Diocese priest pleaded guilty to molesting a female parishioner and molesting three others as part of a deal with prosecutors.

- Mrs. Shirley Baxter, who went deer hunting with her husband, is very proud that she was able to shoot a fine buck as well as her husband.

- Brendan O'Leary, 14, knows the red quebracho tree grows in Bolivia and that it's used to tan leather, off the top of his head.

- In 1994, Gravano received a five-year prison term for plotting 19 murders in exchange for his cooperation.

- In addition, 700,000 acres now irrigated by ancient methods and yielding but one crop a year could be brought to yield two crops in three years.

- The body was found in an alley by a passerby with a bullet in his head.

- A 27-year-old Stanford student pleaded guilty to the charge of attempting to lure a 10-year-old girl into a sexual liaison in San Mateo Superior Court Friday.

- The suspect was spotted in a vehicle matching the description of one that had been stolen from the Anabelle area by Sheriff's Office Sgt. Craig White.

- Organ donations from the living reached a record high last year, outnumbering donors who are dead for the first time.

- We have been encouraging people to drive to the gym, change clothes, and work out for 20 years.

- A six-year-old dog named Rosie has been honored by the American Humane Association for saving the life of her iron-lung-bound owner during a power outage with gifts of plaques and flowers and all the dog biscuits she could eat.

- The burglar was about 30 years old, white, 5'10", with wavy hair weighing about 150 pounds.

- Conviction for manslaughter carries a penalty of 1 to 10 years in California.

- Already wheezing and short of breath, the principles of sound mountaineering were forgotten as they began their retreat.

- Tens of thousands of New York doctors will learn of biological and chemical terrorism attacks from their e-mail accounts in a program designed to speed up response to bioterror, Gov. George Pataki announced Thursday.

- Avoid the traffic by using one of the park's shuttle buses and view the elk rutting with a park ranger.

- The male body was spotted by a passerby lying in a North. Langley ditch about 9:00 A.M.

- Beginning with three games on Tuesday, the unmistakable drama of postseason baseball will grip all of us who love the game for a month.

- Despite its dismal record in human rights, the House of Representatives has granted most favored nation status to China.

- Residents will be given information on how to reduce the amount of garbage they generate in the form of lectures, printed literature, and promotional items.

- Furrow, a member of the neo-Nazi Aryan Nations with a history of mental problems, surrendered to FBI agents in Las Vegas the day after the shootings.

- I met him before he died two or three times.
- On Thursday, the Kilshaws were served with papers ordering them to appear before an Arkansas court accused of abducting the girls and deceiving officials in the U.S. and Britain.
- As a company that operates throughout the world selling food products, you can well imagine that the most important thing for us is that we operate off a high moral and ethical plane.
- Rubber tile is limited to only a few colors and patterns, but you'll see increased use of it in modern kitchens because its softness and studded surface prevent slipping. Extremely durable and long-lasting, you can expect a life span of up to 20 years.
- Fire broke out on the prairie near the C. P. R. viaduct on Monday evening, but the blaze was extinguished before damage could be done by the local fire brigade.
- She handed out brownies to children wrapped in Tupperware.
- Mr. Johnson has a stack of complaints against the company that is nine feet high.
- Scientists are compiling a database of over one million biological hazards at Virginia Tech.
- Taped to the supply cabinets that line the walls behind a cluttered table, Sharon Olds has put the dreams of her students on display.
- *From medical instructions given out by a urologist in Melbourne, Florida:* You may experience a burning sensation when you urinate for 24 hours.
- She screamed, "Let me go!" and struck the man in the face with a key chain that had a small padlock given to her by her husband that was attached.
- Hunting can also be dangerous, as in the case of pygmies hunting elephants armed only with spears.
- Living in the richest country on Earth, God has richly blessed us.
- Police and child welfare authorities have been publicizing the dangers of leaving a small child in a hot car for more than a decade.
- Place three drops in left eye every two hours while awake for five days.

- Interest in the club has greatly increased due to recent media coverage of Mars, which was as close to Earth as it gets on Thursday.
- Her mother and I tried multiple things to encourage her to read with no success.
- Police searched into the night for a man armed with a shotgun that walked into a Boulder pharmacy Thursday morning, demanded drugs, and then fled.
- Marcia Gerry was charged with DWI, operating a motor vehicle with a blood-alcohol level greater than .1 percent, and unlawful possession of marijuana.
- An ethnically diverse crowd of about 50 gathered at the Falkirk Mansion in San Rafael yesterday for a speakout against hate crimes organized by the Marin County Human Rights Roundtable.
- Children shall not drive golf carts under the age of 16.

THE HALL OF FAME
OF MISPLACED MODIFIERS

- Plunging one thousand feet into the gorge, we saw Yosemite Falls.
- Jewel certainly has made her mark by being perhaps the first folksinger to regularly take the stage with her guitar in four-inch heels and a miniskirt.
- The Diamondbacks' starter was facing a man who can knock any pitch he can reach over the fence.
- After years of being lost under a pile of dust, Chester D. Thatcher III found all the old records of the Bangor Lions Club at Bangor House.
- LOST: A walking stick by an elderly man with a curiously carved ivory head.
- Edwin Newman, author of two Book-of-the-Month Club books on the abuse of language, hinted in a speech to nearly 1,300 persons in Memorial Union Theater that efforts to improve language may be the result of attacks on pompous, weird language such as his.

Taylor Frey led the Cougars with eight tickles.

Typo Negative

An ABC news show ran a story about the reappointment of Alan Greenspan as Federal Reserve chairman. Unfortunately, Greenspan was unable to attend the reappointment ceremony because he had been hospitalized by an enlarged prostate gland. A ribbon crawling across the bottom of the screen announced that Greenspan had stayed home because of "an enlarged prostitute." Commented Greenspan's wife, Andrea Mitchell, "He should be so lucky!"

"It is nearly as hard to correct a typographical error as it is to get a woman unpregnant," wrote a grizzled newspaper editor long ago.

The real-life examples that follow are the kinds of typographical terrors that turn newspaper editors into typochondriacs.

• Gearty said he and Sjolberg talked with Norton about five minutes trying to persuade him to put his gnu down, but he kept the officers covered.

• Proud of her canning abilities, Mrs. Hawkins took Reverend Williams to the basement and showed him her well-filled panties.

• It is rumored here in Hollywood that the film company bought the rights to a new navel for Audrey Hepburn.

• Diane's wedding drew a terrific crowd, including Sally Bates, who everybody thought was a broad.

• Mr. And Mrs. Walter F. Hill announce the coming marriage of their daughter Helene. No mate has been selected for the wedding.

• They were married and lived happily even after.

• Mrs. Winston Churchill told members of the YWCA committees in Liverpool: "Ninety percent of the mistresses at the YMCA hostel beds are not fit to sleep on."

• For the second year in a row, she made the list as one of the ten best-breasted women in the United States.

• Knowles had been in a hospital for the last month as a habitual alcoholic. Police issued orders for hish arrest.

• The Taliban Bakhtar news agency said Abdul Haq was executed because he was spaying for Britain and the United States.

• Ms. Harrison will graduate with a major in piano and a minor voice.

• One way to maintain students' interest is assing them meaningful homework.

• Explore the magical and mysterious world of mountain loins with Mike Middleton from the Division of Wildlife.

• An eight-and-a-half-pound daughter came to frighten the home of Mr. and Mrs. White.

• After 24–48 hours' filtration, the pool becomes so clear that when the water is calm, you can read "heads" or "tails" on a dame lying eight feet below the surface.

- Basic economic principles explain that when taxes go up with no corresponding benefits, the long-rage result will probably be worse than anticipated.
- After popular demand from last year, I am sending another e-mail inbiting you to sink your teeth into our next TECH EXPO job fair.
- The Concord entry won the pee-pee hockey championship.
- Come see ducks, deer, turkey, and wild wife.
- Advanced opportunities. Professional training. $350 per week plus bones.
- A man was arrested and charged with felony terroristic threats and possession of a forearm by a convicted felon.
- Sometimes it is scary to try something new like donating blood. But wouldn't it be worth it if you knew you could be saving up to three olives with a single donation?
- Montreal hockey fans will be happy to learn that their star goalie made his first girl in the last few minutes of play.
- Police have appealed for help in finding the mother of an 89-pound newborn baby girl found abandoned in a wicker basket in bushes near a police station.
- Preheat the oven to 450 degrees and place the foot in it. It will be ready to serve in one hour.
- In India, President Clinton toured the ruins of an earthquake, helped raise money for its victims, and was greeted with huge crows and warm applause.
- Last year, Mother Nature hit the mountain with a furry.
- Tennis stars Andre Agassi and Steffi Graf purchased a $23 mansion in Tiburin last year and spend part of their time living there.
- Personable petite SWF, looking to meet a well-balanced SWM, with good old-fashioned valves.
- Kids' menu (served to chicken under 12)
- FINDING REFUGE: Novelist James W. Hall and his wife find refuse in an airy Key Largo house—perfect for tale-telling and striking sunsets.
- The farmers in Annapolis Valley are pleased to announce

that this year there will be an abundance of apples. This is particularly good news, as most of the farmers haven't had a good crap in years.

- Taylor Frey led the Cougars with eight tickles.

- Susan stopped in the middle of the foyer admiring a tall statue of a hideous-looking creature, half man and half breast.

- *Photo caption:* Steven Gartner, one of the sexist U.S. bachelors

- Bradley, Bowdoin's dead of student affairs, opposes censorship of student opinion.

- *In a storefront window:* Facial & Axing

- *At the University of Missouri:* Quite Please! Ph.D. Students Taking Exams

- Seven lawyers have rescued themselves from the legal panel considering possible sanctions against President Clinton for lying under oath during the Monica Lewinsky scandal.

- *On a form instructing people applying for name changes:* You must sing at the end of part C in the presence of a notary public or commissioner. They may charge a small fee for this service.

- The rumor that President Nixon would veto the bill comes from high White House souses.

- A man licking the locks on doorways of apartments on North Pleasant Street was gone when police got there.

- We are always happy to have you sue our facility.

- Arthur Kitchener was seriously burned Saturday afternoon when he came in contact with a high-voltage wife.

- His 23rd gal of the season moves him into third place in all-time scoring.

- After her appearance in the movie *Airport,* distinguished American actress Helen Hayes indicated that she really preferred appearing on Broadway in stag plays.

- Teachers have reported using the cooking arts to support math lessons where students are learning about measurements and fractures.

- The main problem for the older pilot seems to be a lack of ability to keep ahead of the aircraft, which is traveling very fast at 1.350 mph.

- "I drove home steadily, and I felt quite sober," he added, ainaso cmfw shr cm cmfyp.
- Fax your ad copy to Jim at 555-1234. We'll professionally type-set you ad for you.
- If you feel strongly about any particular subject, why not write to the *Gazette* about it? We prefer discussion on local, rather than rational, topics.
- Help us make a better newspaper: We're panning a new community newspaper, and we want your help.

THE TYPO-GRAPHIC HALL OF FAME

- An in-debt discussion of the new tax laws is available by using the order blank in the tax return package.
- He received his graduate degree in unclear physics.
- Would she climb to top of Mr. Everest again? Absolutely.
- A turdey dinner sponsored by the West Lenoir PTA will be held in the school cafeteria from 4:30 until 7:00 P.M. Friday.
- The defendant was charged with carless driving.
- *Entrapment*, starring Sean Connery and Catherine Zita-Jones, is a terrific flick with two entertaining stars out doing themselves to keep us on the edge of our seats.